100 Years of Olympic Music

Chloe,
Opportunity!
Best wishes!
[illegible]
2009

100 Years of Olympic Music

Music and Musicians of the Modern Olympic Games 1896–1996

William K. Guegold, Ph.D.

Golden Clef Publishing–Mantua, Ohio

100 Years of Olympic Music
Music and Musicians of the Modern Olympic Games 1896—1996

Golden Clef Publishing
4365 Dudley Road
Mantua,OH 44255
USA

Printed by Cobb, Inc., P.O. Box 368, Newport, KY 41071, USA

ISBN: 09652371-0-9 $19.95 (US)
Library of Congress Catalog Card No.: 96-94402

Contents

Chapter 6

Dedication

This book is dedicated to my family (wife, Judi and children, Nathan, Anna, Meghan and Bethany) and the memory of my father, Walter W. Guegold, who passed away unexpectedly on April 20, 1995.

An Interview with John Williams

Conductor Laurette, The Boston Pops Orchestra

This interview took place on Friday, December 28, 1995 in Boston, Massachusetts. I attended the premiere of John's new Olympic Theme, *Summon the Heroes*, the previous evening at Symphony Hall. Accompanying me was Laraine Perri, John's producer and a member of the staff at Sony Digital Masterworks, New York.

G: John, thanks for agreeing to meet with us today. I'd like to begin with a question about the Baron de Coubertin, as founder of the modern Olympic Games. He stated that he believed 'music and the mind' should be reunited in an 'allegiance between sport and art.' How do you see the union of these two ideals?

J: I think of music and art as being mind/spiritual and sport being physical. Those are the dissimilarities. There are strong reflections of artistic or spiritual things that get into athletic performances. They come together in ballet, taking it literally. Ballet is to us at least, all of these. It is athleticism, it is art and it's all this brought together. I saw in *Forbes* magazine a picture of Stefi Graff, stretching for a ball, frozen in a still shot. There is something in this moment that is artistic and poetic as if you could frame it and paint it. And it comes from the reach and all that. It comes from a creature in flight in a way in which she wouldn't have been aware. Plus, there's some sort of spiritual, non-corporal aspect of all of this that gets us close to what art is in some way.

Maybe the other questions relate more to that too, about the continuities of myth and all of this that we all resonate and share. That we respond to when we see people crossing the finish line, busting their gut to do something that doesn't make any sense.

G: We see some of the connection in skating on ice or on a gym mat. The competitors that really strike me are the ones who have done a good job of coordinating their actual moves with the music… or better at expressing the music through their movement.

J: Yes, bringing it closer to ballet. I guess it speaks to what he meant by bringing the physical and artistic things together… of the mysteries of meter and tempo. Athletes probably say, you know like musicians, if you get something in exactly the right pocket, it's not fast, it's not slow, you've hit just the right tempo. That is the secret of all performance. You can talk about dynamics, but dynamics will happen right if the pocket is there. If that kinetic thing is right. And certainly athletes have the same thing. If the tempo is right, if your feet are hitting the ground at the right speed, you'll make the numbers. So I think it's all to do with the cosmic throbbing of mother nature's heart. These are the things that unite athleticism with art.

G: Your brilliant work in film scoring has made you the most visual composer in the world today. Do you find similarities in writing programmatic music for the Olympics—an event rich in visual imagery, you mentioned the TV coverage and stadium venue—and writing film music? What connections or dissimilarities do you find in writing for the different type of media in which you will hear your music performed?

J: I think, it seems to me, that all composers should be (even if they aren't) interested in doing film music. They never used to be. There used to be this snob thing, even Stravinsky, alas, they couldn't get him to write for film and he would have been fantastic. And he was living right there in Hollywood. But I think that's changing. If you go around to the conservatories, the young people want to come to this. This idea of 'audiovisual,' shouldn't be unnatural to musicians, although the purist will say if you want to play Beethoven, you don't want to have any visual aids, why distract the eye. And I'm aware of that problem and that contradiction. But if you can get around that, just as music seems right in athleticism and in tempo—all the things we talked about earlier, it seems to be very right to accompany beautiful things that you can see. It may not be the highest level of musical art when you want to put it in abstract, absolute musical terms and not have visual distractions, but I live with the visual distraction every day and they usually cover up whatever good phrases I can conjure (or if the horses hooves don't cover them up on the soundtrack). But I'm attracted to it because it's a source of rich imagery in the visual sense and in the spooky mythological sense that we feel.

There is pageantry and history in film. You can do a horrible film about Richard III, but you get the Chavalard's, and the flags and the trumpets and all this history that we seem to remember and the way we remember mythology and resonate with it… and you get to blow sixteen trumpets in Hollywood and accompany the flags. This sense of history and heraldic things and pageant things, you can get an almost adolescent turn-on with these things in the film world that is fun for a composer and can provide an inspiration for him. That may connect with the Olympic kind of pageant and all of that.

But then we talked earlier about television and media. This one hundred-year anniversary is something special. I don't think Baron de Coubertin could have imagined what's happened. What's really happened is that this event has become a really unifying thing around the world, a theme about the oneness of humanity and has meaning for us in so many political and cultural levels of all kinds… very valid, very important.

The media gives us this huge opportunity to communicate this ideal with others. You don't write the same kind of piece that you're going to play for an audience of 1,000 as you're going to play out on the Esplanade for an audience of 250,000. You can still have a lot of notes. It doesn't have to be simple. But it seems to me that the line has to be like a big arc. Rather than a lot of pointillistic little aspects of expression. So, I think the media is involved. What we think of Olympic and pageant music has developed a certain kind of idiom that is partly the result of the cross-cultural thing we're doing, the size of the audience, and the reach of it all.

G: Last night, during the concert at Symphony Hall as we were listening to the premiere of *Summon the Heroes,* I had to think that the antiphonal brass seemed to fit the nature of the piece so well. What was it in '84? We had something like 1,000 piano players… I see this new piece with a lot of brass players, in an antiphonal settings… it's a 'stadium' piece. It seems like it will fit so well in that big setting.

J: We could easily expand it. We used eight offstage trumpets (last night). It could be 40 if Dolbian complexities wouldn't wreck it. But if there is a way to keep it in sync, you could certainly do it. I was worried about that in the hall a little bit. We've done things before. Those balconies are fairly low so you can almost get a sense of the distance. It's not like Carnegie Hall, where you can almost touch the boxes. But it's close enough and antiphonal brass, well, there just isn't anything else better than that for calling armies together.

G: Including *We're Lookin' Good*, which was composed for the 1987 Special Olympics International Summer Games, you've now written four pieces for the games. I also note that you composed a piece called *Winter Games* for the 1989 World Ski Championships. It's obvious to me that you've captured the 'Olympic Spirit' in all of your Olympic commissions and, in particular, your new piece. What do you try to communicate in these pieces? We've continued to come back to the mythical/spiritual. Is that what you think of? I guess, we're asking if you write having been inspired by the Olympics or do you write to inspire?

J: These athletes are all very young, you know. Maybe not all of them… is there a "senior Olympic tour? Maybe that's something they should add. But let's assume that they are all kids of 18–22. So the music that would inspire them would be some sort of rock 'n roll that I wouldn't even know about. I don't know if it would work the other way around, if I could inspire them in a way that they could connect with. I hadn't thought about that. So I guess, it's the other way around. The inspiration for me, I guess just comes from the mythological idea that we all seem to feel. It's all about deities and heroes that lived up in the mountains somewhere that could do something we couldn't do. But that there is an unbroken line of knowledge that goes from generation to generation like a fireside folk tradition. I guess the source of all or most folk tradition is mythology. The source of most art is folk art. So the source of art has to be mythology really in the end that we have to know about these people, our parents. The heroes. So that's what it is for me. I guess that's why trumpets. I suppose there are other ways to do it, but I just don't know them. Another generation may have better ways to do it electronically. I really think there is this unbroken mythological thing. Any artistic aspirant must sense that. Don't you think we all do? When we talked about performance before, when you get everything right on the right rail we all know it, we all know when it's right and we know when it's not right. It's not linguistic. It's not intellectual. It's not even visceral. It's spiritual.

The other strong connection, and I think it probably goes back to an earlier question, is this thing about the similarity between athletes, dancers, and musicians in that to begin with there is a lot of practice. That's a word every musician understands and athlete understands. You've got to practice everyday. And if you don't practice everyday you can't win the race and you can't play the concerto. And you loose it. I love that thing. Who was one of the great old time artists that said if I don't practice one day I know it and if I don't practice two days the public knows it. And if I don't practice three days the critics know it. But that has to be the same thing with the athletes. It must be. And these games are also contests and that relates to music in as such that it is contrapuntal competition—that's the whole essence I suppose of polyphony if you want to reason it out that way. Or a concerto, which is a competition between a soloist and this huge unbeatable force. So there are similar things happening with it. So I think in musical terms it's heroes or things like that which we want to write about in the music.

P: I'm curious, with *Summon the Heroes* if you were trying to communicate something markedly different than the other Olympic pieces. If you had a different idea. We're saying they all bring out these similar thoughts, the mythical and the spiritual, but were you trying to do something different with this piece?

J: I think the real thematic thing is a unified singular idea. This one is a bit different. I don't think you can say form, because that is too grand a word, but this one is in five sections in my mind at least. There's kind of a fanfare section and then there's kind of a prologue, which is that trumpet tune. And then there's a section that I call "flags" which is color and all that, and then a kind of a contest section and then a parade at the end. So it has, not a narrative, but it's some kind of form that is different than the others. I was thinking about visuals. Instead of working with a story board, which is the way I'm used to working in so many zillion things, to do it backwards, which I love to do also. I've done this a couple of times with Oliver Stone and Spielberg. They'll say 'go write it.' So how it goes and it's rhythms and kinetic ebbs and flows will give them something the score wouldn't have had otherwise. So that was purely practical, the sectionalization of this thing. And then sometimes a practical thing becomes an artistic thing. And it becomes either a blessing or a curse depending on whether it's a good form or it isn't.

I don't think the new piece is too long. I think the shape is about right. You always worry if the material bears that and that's a thing that has to be calculated. It's long for television, but I think it will work because there's that little beginning section with some drum beats. There was a discussion in Atlanta, because before we play this you will have some drummers from all over the world playing this kind of primitive drum. And they may hit the drum just before we play or they may hit the drums at the beginning of the trumpet call. Or we may extend that a little bit so they can participate more. So that was a consideration. But to answer the question again, it didn't change what it's about, which is aspiration.

G: I think the title is quite aptly suited for this piece. From my standpoint as an observer of the Olympics all these years, it really reflects the image of the beginning of the games.

J: I hope so. Good. We've been going around trying all sorts of language. I like the word 'summon.' Somehow it reflects bringing people together. And linguistically it doesn't seem to be a tainted word either through poetic overuse or commonalty.

It's dedicated to a wonderful player (Boston Pops principal trumpet, Tim Morrison). I went over a couple of keys. It could safely be a tone lower. It's in the key of G so on a C trumpet it hovers around top B and C a couple of times. But there's a risk having it up there, just in that tessitura so that when the player gets it you think, wow! It adds an element of drama. If it was lower it wouldn't have that quality. In the score for JFK there is a similar section and some of them miss that… not too many of them, but it is a challenge. They like trying it. E-flat is a key they hate. Perhaps D major would have been better. How do you know?

G: Four of the tracks on this new recording use orchestra with chorus. That seems to add to the grandness and scale of the pieces as well. Your music has always been grand in scale, where appropriate, using prominent brass scoring and a full symphonic sound. You had mentioned that in future generations, there may be some other types of orchestration that can inspire. Do you believe, as a composer, and as comfortable as you are with the medium, that this is what's required to capture the grandeur that we now associate with the term Olympic?

J: That's a marvelous question because it speaks to this generational thing; about the aptness of this or that medium of expression. Things that we are deeply moved by, our children will perhaps find meaningless. Comedy is perhaps the best example of something that does not travel or translate. If you took the great comedians of 100 years ago and did the

Billy Crystal stand-up of 1890, you'd say 'what is he talking about?' That has to be timely to be funny. And what's funny in one decade isn't in the next and it's that perishable. I think in this area it's less so. I think a symphony orchestra will work for a century's reach, at least. But for where I am, at my age, the symphony orchestra and chorus seems the ideal mediums of expression for this kind of thing. But I can certainly see possibilities with electronics. I use very little electronics in the film scores. When I was studying music these things didn't exist and I'm not computer housebroken in any way. I guess I'm too old to go back over that ground or I've become so comfortable with the acoustic field that it's 'my bag' as the kids would say. I know there are others who are trained in electronics and love it in a way that I don't feel so much.

That's part of the answer. But the other thing is that there is something about trumpets and drums. We talk about Lincoln and one of his great speeches and he mentions the 'mystic chords of memory.' These things that we remember, these unbroken threads, include among them drums—drums of war and a very close second the shepherd's flute and a close third trumpets—trumpets and drums of war, of celebration, of pageantry, of weeping. So, while I'm willing to grant the relative aspect to the relevance of acoustic symphony orchestra material and sung chorus.

That's only part of the answer. The answer in part is that we need drums, we need trumpets or shofars or conch shells or something to blow those fifths.

G: The Bernstein *Olympic Hymn* is something of a discovery. It's interesting to note that Bernstein wrote this piece at the request of the German Olympic Committee and the theme is taken from the finale of his *1600 Pennsylvania Avenue*.

J: We're learning the piece. It's in 5/4 and it's half note, three quarters, unrelentingly so. I began to think that if we sang the half really long and have the three quarters lead us to the next half note, so that there is a lovely curve to the shape. We've looked at some ideas with the balance. Some thinning of the thick divisi in the chorus and a few things we yet want to do with it in rehearsal will make it more clear, more beautiful. It's very 'Sondheimian' and very sweet. It's quite lyric and this must not go unnoticed.

G: Would you consider this a signature Bernstein piece? Will people hear this and say, 'Oh, yea. That's Lenny.'

J: Well, I think it is a signature piece. It belongs to the body of music similar to *Let This Garden Grow* and Copeland's *Tender Land*. Maybe it's a tantalizing idea of an American choral/orchestral tradition that these fellows were starting to get around. It's food for thought.

G: I'm pleased to see included in your selections for the *Summon the Heroes* CD, the Shostakovich *Festive Overture,* which was performed at the 1980 Games in Moscow yet was written in 1954 to commemorate the 37th anniversary of the Russian Revolution. The Suk piece also was not composed specifically for the Olympics. Yet, each selection played a role in the games. Can you discuss what it is about these pieces that makes them Olympic in spirit?

J: I agree with you that these seem to belong and fit right in as Olympic pieces. I'm really enchanted with the Suk, it's a dandy little piece. So that's one thing. It was difficult, as Laraine knows, to find just the kind of repertoire we wanted for this CD. You would think that over 100 years and twenty-five or whatever games we've had, one would have thought that there would have been more similar material there. What we have to think of is this modern revival of the tradition is something that is just starting. One century really isn't all that long and I imagine if we had a meeting like this one hundred years from now we'd probably have a lot more tunes we could put in there.

G: I've done the Suk piece with antiphonal brass and splitting the group side to side. It seems to be another good 'stadium' piece.

J: I think people in this part of the world will be grateful to hear this work. It's quite an attractive piece with a nice face on it.

G: You've included several pieces here that, although they were not performed at an actual Olympic event, seem to exhibit an Olympic flavor or were used in films about the Olympics. Could you discuss the two Vangelis pieces, Rosza's *Parade of the Charioteers* and the *O Fortuna* movement from Orff's *Carmina Burana*?

J: The Vangelis pieces are both film works and there is a definite heroic quality to both, they seem to have that feeling about them. Although they are synthesizer pieces, we have good orchestrations of them and they were hugely popular when we did them with the Pops when the movies came out. Vangelis sort of crosses that line between pop and orchestral music. It is orchestratable and can be brought into a conventional setting. It a good artistic choice.

P: It's interesting to see a piece like the Rosza *Parade of the Charioteers* juxtaposed with Shostakovich and not in an album of film music.

J: The Rosza is interesting. I mean that's all about Herculean stuff. Another word comes to my mind. There's a pagan aspect to it. And I think that's something you can think about the Carl Orff as well. We talked about atavisms and vague collective memories in this conversation and that paganism has a place in that kind of thing. There's a… that's part of it too, although I'm not sure how. Maybe the part we can be less proud of. It wafts around the spirit of it too. And the feats of Hercules and the slaves in chains and all that spectacle.

G: Torke's *Javelin* was recently commissioned by the Atlanta Committee for the Olympic Games in honor of the Atlanta Symphony Orchestra's 50th Anniversary Season. This selection is considerably different in character than many of the other Olympic pieces. What attracts you, as a composer and conductor, to this piece?

J: It's a commission from Atlanta and should be reflected here. There's a nice tune in there. It's sort of minimalistic and has a style that is good for training montages and all this in athletics that you have to get it right through repetition as well. It's an attractive piece, very well made with wonderful expansion of ideas. It's a long kind of hemiola, if you like, a series of metric things that happen with it. So within the regularity and repetition is a kind of labyrinth of metric things one has to get around in an interesting way. It's a fresh contemporary style.

G: Thanks so much for your time today, John. We all hope that there's a lot more great music coming out of John Williams in the future!

Prelude

The catalyst for this book and its associated research was a performance of Josef Suk's *Toward a New Life* march which I heard on WKSU in Kent, Ohio in 1986 while driving in my car. At the time I didn't know what the selection was and called the station when I arrived at school to ask what the piece was. They were able to provide me with the name, group, and recording particulars. I ordered the Supraphon recording (by the Czech Philharmonic) and soon learned that the march was actually part of a larger three movement work titled *War Tryptic* written just after WWI. The surprise came in reading the jacket notes where it was mentioned that the march was selected Best Music at the 1932 Los Angeles Olympics. That was the first time I had heard any information about music receiving awards at the Olympics.

Although I was very interested in learning more about the Olympics contests, my first inclination was to transcribe the march for band. No mention of a United States publisher was made on the record jacket and I began asking around for information. Just by chance I happened to remember that two of my teaching colleagues at Crestwood High School, where I was band director at the time, knew a gentleman named Jarislav Motlik who played in the Czech Philharmonic. They had met him on an exchange program several years earlier and had corresponded with him on different occasions. He had even written a march and dedicated it to Crestwood High School.

I wrote to him and questioned the possibility of finding a score to use as a basis of the transcription. Several months passed with no word. In the mean time I requested a professional development leave from Crestwood and became the acting assistant director of bands at Kent State University while I completed my Ph.D. coursework. During the Spring of 1987 I was contacted by my colleagues and notified that Jarislav would be in the United States with a tour of the Czech Philharmonic who would be performing at Severance Hall in Cleveland. There was the possibility that he would be able to visit their home during this time.

The three of them were able to visit Kent State during the tour and attend rehearsals of the universities ensembles. Upon arrival at the university, Jarislav presented me with a package that included a copy of the score to *Toward a New Life*. Finally, I was able to complete a transcription (eventually published by Great Works Publishing in Grafton, Ohio in 1992). The march transcription has been performed at the Midwest International Band and Orchestra Clinic by the Gahanna, Ohio High School Band and at the 1994 Music Educators National Conference Professional In-Service held in Cincinnati, Ohio by the United States Army Band, Washington, D.C.

During the period of time that I completed the transcription, the notes describing the awarding of a silver medal to the piece at an Olympics Game continued to haunt me. In 1992, I wrote to the United States Olympic Committee headquarters in Colorado Springs, Colorado to inquire about Olympic Music contests. They were unable to give me any specific information and referred me to the International Olympic Headquarters in Lausanne, Switzerland. The person I contacted there was not versed in many references of Olympic Music, but was able to send me the addresses of all of the past Olympic Games host countries and their local committees.

Slowly information began to arrive and I was able to secure a faculty research grant to travel personally to Lausanne and visit the new Olympic Museum in August of 1993. I also had the good fortune to make contact with the Amateur Athletic Foundation Museum in Los Angeles, California. The Vice President of Research and Library Services, Dr. Wayne Wilson, was a tremendous help in providing references they had collected in Los Angeles following the 1984 Games.

As of the first printing of this manuscript, I have collected more than 1,000 pages of materials, 30 recordings, several videotapes, and numerous letters. These, coupled with countless hours of phone calls, faxes, and direct contacts from all over the world, have resulted in the work you have before you.

ACKNOWLEDGMENTS

I would also like to thank the many people who have helped with the research leading up to the publication of this material. Of tremendous help was Dr. Wayne Wilson of the Amateur Athletic Museum and Foundation, Los Angeles, California. Wayne was always as close as a phone call and was able to send me on many successful leads. Andrea Olivera, on the library staff at the new Olympic Museum in Lausanne, Switzerland, was most pleasant to work with during my visit there in 1993.

Special information was provided by people from many of the past Olympic host countries including Harry Gordon (Australia), Kaisa Laitinen (Sports Museum Foundation of Finland), Sylvia Doucette (Canadian Olympic Association), Guillemette Hybois (French Olympic Committee), P. Thiurman (Netherlands Olympic Committee), S. Smirnova (Media Director, Russian Olympic Committee), and Toru Ushikoshi (NAOC Planning and Finance Section, Japan).

Dr. Joseph Navari and Dr. Mary Shiller (University of Akron), Pastor Douglas Riley (Christ Lutheran Church, Mantua), and Marcie McGaughey (Germany) all worked on numerous translations, without which this book would have been impossible.

Cindy Slater at the United States Olympic Headquarters in Colorado Springs, Colorado, was extremely helpful in pointing me in the right direction after my initial inquiries in 1991.

I would also like in thank Bucky Johnson, director of the 1996 Atlanta Olympic Band, for providing current progress of the musical program in Atlanta. David Bressler of New York City was generous in loaning me copies of Olympic music he has collected.

The short time I spent in Boston to observe the premiere of John Williams' new Olympic Theme, *Summon the Heroes*, and to interview him was certainly enhanced by Laraine Perri, John's producer. We also spent many hours on the phone and faxing information back and forth to prepare the program notes for the CD and the interview with John.

A very special thanks goes to the most gracious John Williams for permitting me the opportunity to interview him in December of 1995. His warm and personable demeanor helped put me a ease and made the interview a most enjoyable experience.

The University of Akron deserves my gratitude for issuing me a faculty research grant in August of 1993 to travel to Lausanne, Switzerland and spend a week at the IOC Library and Museum.

And finally, I must give a great deal of the credit for the realization of this book to Dana Elkin. Dana is a former high school student of mine, currently completing her masters degree in music education here at the University of Akron. I am certain that when she accepted our offer for a teaching assistantship she had no idea this project would be waiting. She has been a fantastic editor, graphic designer, and friend.

WKG

History of the Olympics

Ancient Olympic Games

Every four years in Olympia, Greece from 776 B.C. through 393 A.D.

Modern Summer Olympic Games

Olympiad	*Year*	*Location*	*Dates*
I	1896	Athens, Greece	April 6–15
II	1900	Paris, France	May 20–October 28
III	1904	St. Louis, Missouri, USA	July 1–November 23
IV	1908	London, Great Britain	April 27–October 31
V	1912	Stockholm, Sweden	May 5–July 22
VI	1916	Berlin, Germany	canceled because of WWI
VII	1920	Antwerp, Belgium	April 20–September 12
VIII	1924	Paris, France	May 4–July 27
IX	1928	Amsterdam, Holland	May 17–August 12
X	1932	Los Angeles, California, USA	July 30–August 12
XI	1936	Berlin, Germany	August 1–16
XII	1940	Tokyo, Japan; Helsinki, Finland	canceled because of WWII
XIII	1944	London, Great Britain	canceled because of WWII
XIV	1948	London, Great Britain	July 29–August 14
XV	1952	Helsinki, Finland	July 19–August 3
XVI	1956	Melbourne, Australia	November 22–December 8
XVII	1960	Rome, Italy	August 25–September 11
XVIII	1964	Tokyo, Japan	October 10–24
XIX	1968	Mexico City, Mexico	October 12–27
XX	1972	Munich, Germany	August 26–September 10
XXI	1976	Montreal, Canada	July 17–August 1
XXII	1980	Moscow, USSR	July 19–August 3
XXIII	1984	Los Angeles, California, USA	July 28–August 12
XXIV	1988	Seoul, South Korea	August 23–September 16
XXV	1992	Barcelona, Spain	July 25–August 9
XXVI	1996	Atlanta, Georgia, USA	July 19–August 4
XVII	2000	Sidney, Australia	September 16–October 1

Modern Winter Olympic Games

Olympiad	*Year*	*Location*	*Dates*
I	1924	Chamonix, France	January 25–February 4
II	1928	St. Moritz, Switzerland	February 11–19
III	1932	Lake Placid, New York, USA	February 4–15
IV	1936	Garmisch-Partenkirchen, Germany	February 6–16
	1940	Sapporo, Japan; St. Moritz, Switzerland; Garmisch-Partenkirchen, Germany	canceled because of WWII
	1944	Cortina D'Ampezzo, Italy	canceled because of WWII
V	1948	St. Moritz, Switzerland	January 30–February 8
VI	1952	Oslo, Norway	February 14–25
VII	1956	Cortina D'Ampezzo, Italy	January 26–February 5
VIII	1960	Squaw Valley, California, USA	February 18–28
IX	1964	Innsbruck, Austria	January 29–February 9
X	1968	Grenoble, France	February 6–18
XI	1972	Sapporo, Japan	February 3–13
XII	1976	Innsbruck, Austria	February 4–15
XIII	1980	Lake Placid, New York, USA	February 14–23
XIV	1984	Sarejevo, Yugoslavia	February 7–19
XV	1988	Calgary, Canada	February 13–28
XVI	1992	Albertville, France	February 8–23
XVII	1994	Lillehammer, Norway	February 12–27
XVIII	1998	Nagano, Japan	February 7–22
XIX	2002	Salt Lake City, Utah, USA	February 8–24

"The important thing in the Olympic Games is not to win but to take part, the important thing in life is not the triumph but the struggle. The essential thing is not to have conquered but to have fought well. To spread these precepts is to build up a stronger and more valiant and, above all, more scrupulous and more generous humanity."

Baron Pierre de Coubertin

1

Overview

Even in the ancient Olympic Games writers, sculptors, and artists came to be inspired and to inspire.

In classic Greek times, both art and music were incorporated into the Games. Many athletes exercises were accompanied by flute music as noted on paintings of the period. The poet Pindar (520–445 BC) was commissioned to write ceremonial hymns with which the victors were honored. In his tenth Olympic ode, he writes:

All the precinct rang with music
sung at the feat
In the mode of praise

The ancient Olympic Games were held every four years from 776 BC to 393 AD. In 1894 Baron Pierre de Coubertin sought to reintroduce the Olympic Games to modern society. He was a French historian, journalist, and social critic who sought to reform the French educational system by infusing it with ideas and methods already in practice in England. Baron Pierre de Coubertin's goal in reinstating the Olympics was "to reunite in the bonds of legitimate wedlock a long-divorced couple—Muscle and Mind" by creating an allegiance between Sport and Art in the Olympic Games.

In the 1995 August/September *Olympic Review,* Geoffroy De Navacelle states that "he (de Coubertin) was astonishingly talented in many areas, particularly art, which explains his wish to associate art and culture with Olympism and its manifestations… Similarly, the appearance of harps on stage at the Sorbonne in 1894 as part of the musical programme can be explained by Peirre's love for music (he was an excellent pianist himself, without learning music theory, just as he obtained a law degree without attending classes.)"

In 1894 de Coubertin organized a group of like-minded people which became the first Olympic Congress. At that meeting the group heard the *Hymn to Apollo* set to music by Gabriel Fauré and sung by Jeanne Remacle and several choirs. This group organized the first modern Olympic Games of 1896 in Athens, Greece.

After the 1896 Games, de Coubertin wrote that

> *"Fashions have undergone many changes over two thousand years, but music has remained the factor which best conveys the emotion within a crowd, and which best accompanies the amplitude of a great spectacle."*

The original Olympic Arts Competitions were to be held on an equal footing with the athletic events. Participants were to be rewarded with bronze, silver, and gold medal awards. This concept was created by the Consultative Conference on Arts, Literature, and Sport in 1906. De Coubertin was greatly influential in seeing that there was a twofold place for the arts in the Olympics: 1) to organize the resounding contribution of art and literature to the modern Olympic Games, and 2) to bring about their modest participation, on a day-to-day basis, at local sporting events.

In de Coubertin's Pedagogie Sportive, Switzerland (1919), he stated that "Sport must be seen as producing beauty and as an opportunity for beauty. It provides beauty because it creates the athlete, who is a living sculpture. It is an opportunity for beauty through the architecture, the spectacles, and the celebrations which it brings about."

It was at the 1906 Consultative Conference in Paris that the Baron and his appointees from people of wealth and prestige met to discuss the extent that the Arts and Letters could associate themselves with the Modern Olympiad. Architecture, dramatic art, choreography, decoration, letters, music, painting, and sculpture were to be considered as they were directly inspired by the idea of sport. They also discussed ways in which open-air plays, processions, and props as well as lighting effects might enhance the atmosphere of the Games.

De Coubertin wrote in his 1910 essay *A Modern Olympia* that he wanted future Olympiads (three had been held to date) to be "endowed with refinement and beauty." He was aware of the efforts of countryman Émile Jaques-Dalcroze who was making an attempt to reform music education by combining dance/movement with music. It was obvious to de Coubertin that when Dalcroze united movement, music, and lighting effects it had an incredible effect on audiences and might have a place in his Olympic Games.

He did recognize the uniqueness of the arts in a competitive nature and noted in his Suggestions To Competitors of 1912 (Olympic Review—1911) that "however it is treated, art cannot be ruled the same way as sport." Despite some degree of concern about the judging methods, competitions in architecture, city planning, sculpture, painting, music, and literature were conducted from 1912 through 1948. Dramatic plays were entered as part of the literature category. These contests were held seven times, associated with each Olympic Games during this period (three were canceled due to world wars in 1916, 1940, and 1944).

As you will read in the following chapter, many of these contests were less than successful even though many of the associated Fine Arts Exhibitions were attended by large numbers of people. The Los Angeles festival held as part of the 1932 Games occupied 15 galleries and included 1,100 exhibits of paintings, drawings, sculptures, architectural designs, and decorative arts, and drew crowds in the neighborhood of 384,000 people.

2

Arts Competitions

The arts competitions were held under the direct auspices of the International Olympic Committee (IOC) and not the host Organizing Committee as the costs of these events were deemed to be prohibitive. The eventual demise of the music contests in particular was due to the cost of hiring musicians (or full symphonic orchestras) to play the numerous entrant's works that may never be performed again. Also, composers of adequate standing preferred to serve on the adjudication panels rather than submit works. In fact, in 1924 no prizes were awarded and only Josef Suk's *Toward a New Life* won a silver medal in 1932. After 1936 the musical works were divided into several distinct categories.

The first composer to win a gold medal in music was Italian, Ricardo Barthelemy, in 1912 for his *Triumphal Olympic March*.

Synopsis of Olympic Medals in Music

Vth Olympiad		
Stockholm (1912)		
Gold	*Triumphal Olympic March*	Ricardo Barthelemy (Italy)
VIIth Olympiad		
Antwerp (1920)		
Gold	*Olympique*	G. Monier (Belgium)
Silver	*Epinicion*	Oreste Riva (Italy)
IXth Olympiad		
Amsterdam (1928)		
Bronze	*Hellas*	Rudolf Simonsen (Denmark)
Xth Olympiad		
Los Angeles (1932)		
Silver	*Toward a New Life*	Josef Suk (Czechoslovakia)
XIth Olympiad		
Berlin (1936)		
Songs:		
Gold	*Olympischer Schwur*	Paul Hoffer (Germany)
Silver	*Kantate zur Olympiade 1936*	Kurt Thomas (Germany)
Bronze	*Der Laufer*	Harald Genzmer (Germany)
Orchestral Compositions:		
Gold	*Olympische Festmusik*	Werner Egk (Germany)
Silver	*Il vincitore*	Lino Liviabella (Italy)
Bronze	*Bergsuite*	Jaroslav Krika (Czechoslovakia)
XIVth Olympiad		
London (1948)		
Songs:		
Bronze	*Olympic Hymn*	Gabriele Bianchi (Italy)
Instrumental Compositions:		
Silver	*Divertimento for Flute and Streicher*	Jean Weinzweig (Canada)
Bronze	*Toccata for Klavier*	Sergio Lauricella (Italy)
Choral and Orchestra Compositions:		
Gold	*Olympijska Symphony*	Zbrigniew Turski (Poland)
Silver	*Barenjagd for Orchestra*	Kalervo Tuukanen (Finland)
Bronze	*Kraft for Orchestra*	Erling Brene (Denmark)

3

Music and Protocol in Olympic Ceremonies

The truly official functions of the Olympic Ceremonies are the opening and closing ceremonies of the Games and the awarding of medals. Emphasis is made of the athletes taking the Olympic Oath, the awarding of the winners medals, and the opening ceremonies. The Olympic Flag became an integral part of the ceremonies and functions of the Games in 1920, having been designed by de Coubertin in 1913 and approved by the Olympic Congress in 1914. The Flame symbolizes the athletes desire for perfection and struggle for victory. It was introduced for the first time in 1928 at the Games held in Amsterdam. It was in 1936 that the tradition of carrying the torch from Olympia to the host stadium, began with the event becoming a regular part of the Winter Games as well in 1964. The releasing of doves has been an official part of the Games since 1920.

An official Olympic Hymn remains a contentious subject even today. Although the Hymn by Spiros Samaras was officially adopted in 1958, host Organizing Committees, countries, and even television networks have attempted to introduce new theme songs as well as new official hymns. Every year there seems to be a desire in Olympic circles for a new work that truly symbolizes the Olympic spirit. Since 1960 the official hymn has been the Samaras version, although each Organizing Committee has had the privilege of commissioning a theme song to be used as a integral part of the musical presentations of the respective Games.

Synopsis of Olympic Hymns and Their Composers

Athens (1896)	*The Olympic Hymn*	Spiros Samaras (music), Kostis Palamas (text)
Paris (1900)	No designated hymn	
Saint Louis (1904)	No designated hymn	
London (1908)	No designated hymn	
Stockholm (1912)	*Triumphant Olympic March*	H. Alexandersson
Antwerp (1920)	*Olympic Hymn*	Pierre Benoit
Paris (1924)	*Deux Choeurs*	Tourcoing (Prague)
Amsterdam (1928)	*Chant du Drapeau*	Gerrit van Weezel
Los Angeles (1932)	*Olympic Hymn*	Bradley Keeler
Berlin (1936)	*Olympic Hymn*	Richard Strauss
London (1948)	*Non Nobis Domine*	Roger Quilter (music) Rudyard Kipling (text)
Helsinki (1952)	*Olympic Hymn*	Jaakko Linjama (music) Toivo Lyy (text)
Melbourne (1956)	*Olympic Hymn*	Michal Spisak
Rome (1960)	*The Olympic Hymn**	Spiros Samaras, Kostis Palamas (1896 original)

* Adopted as the official Olympic Hymn for all future Games in 1958.

Synopsis of Olympic Themes and Their Composers

Tokyo (1964)	*The Tokyo Olympic Hymn*	Osamu Shimizu, Ron Ogura
Mexico (1968)	*Bugler's Dream*	Leo Arnaud
Munich (1972)	*Olympic Music*	Alfred Goodman
Montréal (1976)	*March of the Athletes*	André Mathieu
Moscow (1980)	*Festive Overture*	Dimitri Shostakovich
Los Angeles (1984)	*Olympique Fanfare*	John Williams
Seoul (1988)	*Hand in Hand*	Moroder and Whitlock
	Olympic Spirit	John Williams (NBC-TV theme)
Barcelona (1992)	*Amigos Para Siempre*	Andrew Lloyd Webber
	The Games	John Tesh (NBC-TV theme)
Lillehammer (1994)		Tamara Kline (CBS-TV theme)
Altanta (1996)	*Summon the Heroes*	John Williams (NBC-TV theme)

It is interesting to note the procedure leading up to the selection of a new official Olympic Hymn for the Games of 1956. The competition was announced in May of 1954 and the judging was to take place at the IOC Congress held in Monte-Carlo from April 18–24, 1955. The winner of the contest would receive a Commemorative Medal from the IOC and $1,000 (provided by Prince Pierre of Monte Carlo). Rules of the contest were rather simple.

There was no age restriction and composers from any country could participate. There were several restrictions concerning the entry deadline (December 20, 1954) and in what manner the piece should be submitted (envelope, etc.). The composition must be strictly original and never have been performed before. The piece should be of hymn-like quality, symphonic in nature, and fit the prescribed text from the Greek poet Pindar. The piece should not exceed four nor be shorter than three minutes.

An international jury was selected to evaluate the compositions. This group included: Nadia Boulanger, Necil Kazim Akses, Vigo N. Bentzon, Doris Blacher, Lennox Berkeley, Pablo Casals, Aaron Copland, Ernesto Halfter, F.G. Malipiero, Frank Martin, N. Nobokof, Ant. Panifnik, Domingo Santa Cruz and A. de Spotzmuller. Boulanger, Malipiero, and Akses served as a preliminary screening committee and reviewed the 387 submitted scores from 39 countries shortly after the deadline. During the final selection meeting in April, all but four of the entries were eliminated. Chavéz, Cruz, and Dimitri Shostakovich (who had not answered an earlier invitation to participate in the judging) were unable to attend. After two days of deliberation, Polish composer Michal Spisak's entry was narrowly chosen as the winner. The new hymn was performed during the session in the Garnier Concert Hall at the Monte-Carlo Casino with both Prince Ranier III and Prince Pierre de Monaco in attendance. The work was given final approval at the 50th Session of the IOC in Paris and introduced to Olympic Competitions in Barcelona (Mediterranean Games of 1955), Cortina (1956 Winter Games), Stockholm (Summer Equestrian Events of 1956), and the Summer Games in Melbourne later in the same year.

The Olympic Oath as envisioned by de Coubertin was a formal means of vowing to uphold the spirit and law of the Olympic Ideal. It was first used in 1920 for the opening of the Antwerp Games.

Playing the winner's national anthem while presenting the flag of the medalists has been an integral part of the Games since the beginning. There has been definite conjecture expressed that such show of nationalistic pride detracts from the global spirit that participation in the Games is supposed to embody. Yet, for participants and spectators alike, this ceremony remains one of the most stirring aspects of the Games and in many cases is, emotionally, a close second to the actual winning of an event.

Specific details of opening and closing ceremonies are at the discretion of the host country Organizing Committees. They are encouraged to plan as extravagant and varied a program as their finances and other resources permit. The IOC restricts certain aspects of the program including a prescribed order for the opening ceremonies. First, the sovereign head of state is introduced to the stadium spectators. This is followed by the parade of athletes. Each group is to be dressed in an official home country uniform with a placard or shield and national flag introducing the team. Greece, as the original home of the Olympics, always leads the procession followed by the participating countries in alphabetical order with the host country last to enter the stadium.

The chair of the host Organizing Committee then introduces the President of the IOC who in turn asks the head of state to officially open the Games. The Flag is then brought into the stadium and is raised after a somewhat brief fanfare of trumpets. This is followed by a ceremony in which the original 1920 Olympic Flag is transferred from the host mayor of the previous Games to the mayor of the current site. There follows a three-gun salute and the release of the doves. The torch is finally brought into the stadium and remains burning until the end of the Games. At this point an athlete from the host country takes the Olympic Oath for all competitors. A judge also takes the oath on behalf of all the judges. After the athletes recess from the stadium, the host country is then permitted to continue with a gala display of one sort or another.

The closing ceremonies have been traditionally shorter and more simple than the opening. Television broadcasts have had an impact on making both opening and closing ceremonies more visually oriented and longer. Once again the flag bearers march into the stadium, this time followed by only six representatives of each competing team intermingled six to ten abreast (the athletes have revised this procedure spontaneously from time to time and the number of team members varies greatly with the norm currently including the entire team). This is followed by the playing of the current host's national anthem and the anthem of the next host country. The President of the IOC then closes the Games. A fanfare is played, the flame extinguished, and the flag slowly lowered and carried from the stadium. After a five-gun salute, the athletes leave the grounds. This can be followed by another gala celebration usually highlighting the cultures of the host country. The tradition of featuring the cultural aspects of the host countries can be traced back to the Games of 1912. In recent years, the closing ceremonies have become more spectacular and the athletes have chosen to remain in the stadium and participate in the postlude festivities.

In 1912 at the Stockholm Games, an Entertainments Committee was formed to arrange for several events, including concerts, dance performances, and theater shows to be given during the course of the Games. The Royal Opera performed six operas: *Carmen*, *Romeo and Juliet*, *Tosca*, *Lohengrin*, *The Tales of Hoffman*, and *La Bohéme*. Other productions produced in the area included *A Midsummer Night's Dream*, *Mostellaria*, *The Count of Luxemburg*, *The Merry Widow*, and *Chaste Susanna*.

Special ceremonies reached a pre-WWII peak in Los Angeles in 1932, and Berlin in 1936. In 1932 a pageant called *California Welcomes the World* was produced, especially for visitors and the athletes, by a group called Hostesses of the Tenth Olympiad. In Berlin logistics and technology played an important part in the Games. Through special arrangements of the German Railway, the Postal Service, and the National Socialist Special Guard, 10,000 youngsters were transported to the site. Shortwave radio equipment was used by the stadium director to permit him to move about the stadium and communicate with the various participants. Even the Reich War Ministry provided two antiaircraft batteries from the Air Force to orchestrate a dome of light over the stadium during a performance of Beethoven's Ninth Symphony.

The ceremonies of the London Games of 1948 were not nearly as spectacular as those of prewar Berlin. Art exhibitions were scheduled for London and Helsinki in 1952. These were the only arts components in these two Games and perhaps led to a rethinking of the process by the IOC.

Meeting in Athens in 1954, the IOC Executive Commission, at the request of President Avery Brundage, decided to leave the responsibility for the cultural program to the Organizing Committee for each Games. Of primary importance would be an exhibition of native art work. It was decided that diplomas would be presented to participants rather than medals. This decision was written into the Olympic Charter as Article 31:

> *"The Organizing Committee will organize a demonstration or exhibition of Art (architecture, music, literature, painting, sculpture, sports philately, and photography...)*
> *The program could also include ballets, theater performances, operas or symphony concerts."*

4

The Early Years 1896–1920

Athens, Greece (Summer, 1896)

How it all began.

The first modern Olympic Games came about due to a gift from the wealthy architect Georgios Averoff. This award was supplemented by sales of souvenir stamps and medals. Some reports covering the inaugural Games alluded that the competitors performances were only mediocre, yet the interest for resurrecting such an event was rekindled that year in Athens.

The Greek composer Dionysios Lavrangas (1864–1941) wrote a hymn for choir and orchestra titled *Pentathalon* for the event with the same name. Several musical events took place in this the first of the modern Olympic Games. The Philharmonic Band of Corfu led the parade and a group of singers from the Piraeus Musical Union singing a song titled *The Sailor Lad* followed by the band playing selections from Wagner's *Lohengrin*. Bugle calls were used to announce the assembling for the procession to the stadium. The parade was led by a series of bands including a garrison band, another band from Corfu, the naval band, other bands from Laurion, Leucas, Cephallonia, Zakynthus, and the Philharmonic Band of Athens.

The first official Olympic Hymn was written by the Greek composer, Spiros Samaras with Kostis Palamas providing the text. Samaras was born in Corfu in 1863 and died in Athens in 1917. He studied composition with Enrico Stancabiano in Athens and Delibes at the Paris Conservatory. He is most noted for his operas and operettas.

The Samaras version remained the official Olympic Hymn until 1912 at which time various new hymns were attempted until 1958. His music was retained for the Games of 1960 and continues to be used today at all opening and closing ceremonies.

Paris, France (Summer, 1900)

The 1900 Games in Paris were nearly overshadowed by the World Exhibition being held at the same time and very little exists concerning the music performed at these events.

St. Louis, USA (Summer, 1904)

St. Louis suffered some of the same problems as the previous event in Paris. Only two quite incomplete reports exist from the 1904 Games. These were written by Charles J.P. Lucas

(The Olympic Games 1904) and J.E. Sullivan (Spalding's Official Athletic Almanac for 1905). The Sullivan report is more accurate as he was director of the Games. These Games were unusual for two reasons. They were originally scheduled for Chicago but were moved by the IOC since St. Louis was holding the World's Fair in 1904. The Fair was officially called The Louisiana Purchase Exposition. It lasted more than six months and Sullivan attempted to schedule a sporting event each day of the fair. Every event, whether a sanctioned Olympic event or not, was labeled as such, creating a great deal of confusion regarding the results of the Games. Therefore, Olympic events were only one part of a multitude of activities carried on during this six-month extravaganza.

A Bureau of Music was appointed to coordinate and hire musicians and groups for the event. No records indicate which bands may have played for or during the Olympic events, but it is likely that some were coordinated as there were approximately 1,087 professional band concerts during the 217 days of the fair. No definitive report exists concerning the results of the sporting events.

The many bands that did perform at these Games included some of the most famous professional touring groups of the time. Sousa, Inne, Contorno, Weber, Fanciulli were just a few of the nearly 15 groups to perform. Reports indicate that the musicians were paid well. For example, Sousa's group performed for four weeks and was paid $20,000. The Boston Band performed for 10 weeks and was paid $37,500.

As part of the overall budget for the Bureau of Music, there was a sizable sum dedicated to the commissioning of pieces for the opening ceremonies. This included *Hymn of the West* based on a poem by Clarence Stedman with music set by John Knowles Paine. This was designated as the official World's Fair Hymn. The two other commissioned works were *Louisiana March* by Frank Van der Stucken and *Along the Plaza* waltz by Henry K. Hadley.

London, England (Summer, 1908)

London marked first time that amateurism is specifically defined with certification by the host country and the IOC.

The 1908 Games were to have been held in Rome, but were moved to London when adequate financial arrangements could not be planned. The focus of the events was at Shepherd's Bush Stadium. The trumpeters of the Life Guards played a fanfare to open the Games followed by the British National Anthem performed by the Grenadier Guards. A bugle call signaled the athletes to exit in alphabetical order. One of Irving Berlin's early songs, *Dorando,* which told the story of the Italian marathon runner, was performed at the 1908 Games.

The arts contests were originally scheduled to begin here but had to be put off until Stockholm. Concerts were a part of the social events surrounding the Games with one given in the evening of July 30 at the lawn of a Mr. Foy. The Royal Irish Fusiliers played all week at the town of Henley along the river.

Although these Games were marked by many procedural protests, plans were set into motion for the next one in Stockholm.

Stockholm, Sweden (Summer, 1912)

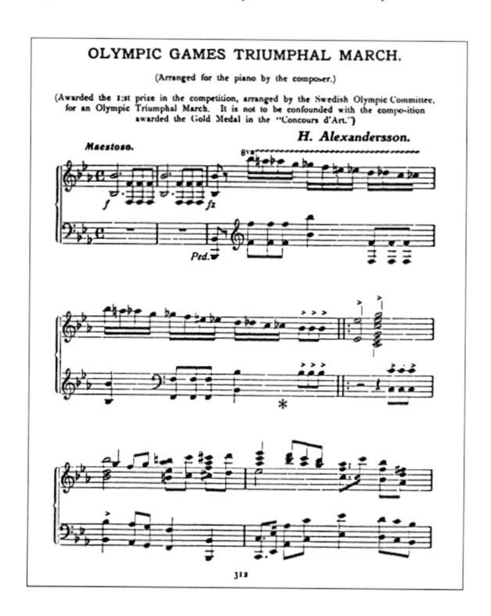

The Stockholm Games were punctuated by firsts. Not only were the first art and literature competitions introduced here, but the first electric timing devices were used. It was also the first time that a public address system was utilized. Unfortunately, unlike ancient times when the Olympics caused wars to be suspended or postponed, the outbreak of WWI led to the suspension of the Games until 1920.

At the opening Olympic Banquet a double quartet of men's voices led by Herr Gentzel performed. Later a men's choir of 2,500 gave a concert. Trumpeters dressed in medieval costumes played a fanfare from the towers after the King's opening speech. The choir of the Swedish Choral Association sang a national air following a cheer for the King. The athletes left the grounds to the *Olympic Games Triumphal March*, composed by Dr. H. Alexandersson. This piece was awarded first prize (gold medal) in a competition held by the Swedish Olympic Committee. Ricardo Barthelemy's Triumphal Olympic March won the gold medal for the music category in the arts competition. This was the first medal awarded in the music contests.

Another popular piece written for these Games was the *Valse Boston for the Olympiska Spelen* by Theodor Pinet and published in Stockholm.

5

Between the Great Wars

Antwerp, Belgium (Summer, 1920)

G. Monier of Belgium received a Silver Medal for his entry in the music competitions. Once again records are sketchy concerning ceremonial music during the Antwerp Games of 1920. Many records were later lost or destroyed during the WWII.

Chamonix, France (Winter, 1924)

The first Winter Games!

No record of music or musicians has been preserved from these Games.

Paris, France (Summer, 1924)

The *Marseillaise* was played during the opening ceremonies. Records are not specific as to what group performed this selection.

The juries for the music part of the arts competitions included Bartók, Gustave Charpentier, Paul Dukas, Enesco, Manuel de Falla, Fauré, Honegger, Vincent D'Indy, Malipiero, Ravél, Albert Roussel, Florent Schmidt, and Stravinsky.

Although the jury was a distinguished one, the same cannot be said about the quality of the entries. Seven individuals from five different countries submitted works, but none were chosen to receive medals. Submissions and their composers included:

Chasse a courre, L. Ruby Reynolds-Lewis (Australia)
Jeux Funeraires, S. Daneau (Belgium)
*Hymne aux Sport*s, Gerry (France)
Ludus pro Patria, Masquillier Thiriez (France)
Marche Sportive pour piano, J. Richard (France)
Now Let the Games Begin, G. Bamber (Great Britain)
Ski-Sporten, M. Moaritz (Norway)

Jules Hubert wrote a piece titled *Les Jeux Olympiques* for these Games. However, records are unclear if it was actually performed during the ceremonies.

St. Moritz, Switzerland (Winter, 1928)

No records of specific music citations were found.

Amsterdam, Netherlands (Summer, 1928)

These Games were marked by the first women being permitted to participate in the track and field events. This was not the first time for women competitors as they were previously permitted to compete in tennis, golf, archery, figure skating, yachting, swimming, and fencing.

Some controversy developed concerning the intention of the arts festival here, but it proceeded anyway. S. Dresden and S. van Milligen served as the working committee members for the music portion of the contests. In order to encourage local artists an open letter titled *What is Olympic Art?* was sent to Dutch artists and the public in general by Jonkheer Jan Freith. The general rules for the contests were drawn up by the General Secretary, Mr. Tellers. These rules were drafted after a great deal of discussion. Separate copies for each of the separate art disciplines were distributed to the Dutch artists and organizations. Extra consideration was given to the foreign artists after a lack of communication between the Dutch Committee for Organizing the Olympic Games and the committees of other countries led to controversy. It was decided that everything from foreign countries would be accepted for both the contests and the exhibits, with the decision for inclusion to be left up to the country from which the work or artist originated.

The international juries for the art competitions were appointed as early as 1926. Baron Schmmelpenninck was appointed at the meeting of the IOC in 1927 to be the chair of the Committee. The advisors and jury members were split up so that each art discipline would be represented.

An exhibition site was chosen in the Municipal Museum. This turned out to be quite a successful choice and much more economical than building a new structure. It should also be mentioned that the exhibit drew a crowd of more than 10,000.

The music section of the competition drew 22 entries from nine countries. Included were five vocal, nine orchestral, and eight solo instrument compositions.

The rules for the music entries called for the work to represent some connection between sport and music. Heroic works or lively works for brass, piano, as well as, club songs and chorales could be considered. Large works for orchestra and choir would be considered if they could be performed at a playing field or stadium. Entries by publishers or commercial undertakings would not be accepted.

Compositions were grouped as follows:

A *Song*—for one or more persons, with or without accompaniment of piano or orchestra

B *Solo instrument*—with or without accompaniment and for instrumental chamber music

C *Orchestra*—for military band or brass band

Prizes could be awarded for the best three works in each of the above categories (gold, silver, and bronze).

The jury consisted of Count Clary (Paris) and Prince Casimir Lubomirski (Krakow) for the IOC and the following international members: Gustave Doret (Switzerland), Sem Dresden (Amsterdam), Professor Dr. Z. Jacimecki (Krakow), Dr. W. Mengelberg (Amsterdam), Marco Labroco (Rome), Gabriel Pierné (Paris), Willem Pijper (Amsterdam), and Professor Dr. Max von Schillings (Berlin).

The works were distributed and read and the consensus of the jury was deemed to be quite clear. The official report of the contests mentioned that the jury was quite disappointed with the quality of the entries. Most of the awards were withheld and only one single work received an average score based on the specified criteria. Only the *Symphony No. 2, Hellas* by Rudolf Simonsen of Denmark, received an award and it was a Bronze Medal in category C (large group). *Op ter Olympiade* written by Joh. P. Koppen was used at the ceremonies as a processional/recessional.

Lake Placid, New York, USA (Winter, 1932)

Five bands submitted bids to become the official band of the 1932 Winter Games. The 21-member Adam's Empire State Band of Albany, New York was awarded the contract. This was one of the last of the Sousa-style professional bands in the U.S. The demise of this type of group has been attributed to the popularity and ease of use of recordings and radio. The group performed in the stadium and arena during competitions where special stands were constructed. At the bob sled run and ski jump areas, space was set aside for the band. Additional music was provided by records played on loud speakers as needed.

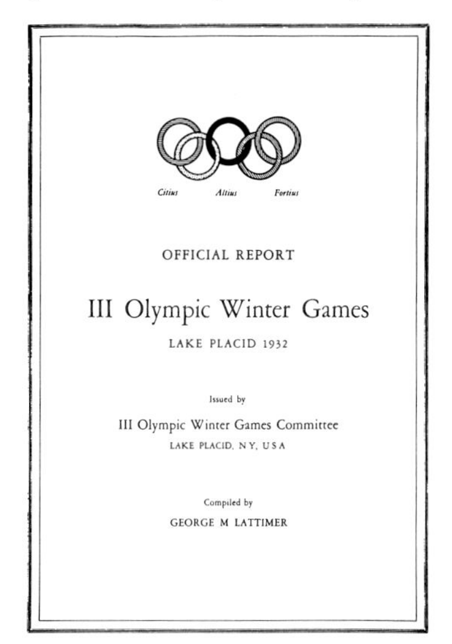

Citius Altius Fortius

OFFICIAL REPORT

III Olympic Winter Games

LAKE PLACID 1932

Issued by

III Olympic Winter Games Committee

LAKE PLACID, N Y, U S A

Compiled by

GEORGE M LATTIMER

Los Angeles, California, USA (Summer, 1932)

Although the Los Angeles Games were held in the midst of the Great Depression, they were quite successful. Firsts for Los Angeles included the use of automatic timing and the camera for photo finishes.

A chorus of 1,200 members was selected and rehearsed for several months before the Games. The chorus performed over the radio on several occasions prior to the Games to help with advertising and promotion. The chorus appeared in the opening and closing ceremonies as well as at the demonstration football game during the Games with the 1,000-member Olympic Band. It is interesting to note that during the football demonstration a drum and bugle corps of 800 joined the massed band and choir providing entertainment and marching drills.

The bands of the 1932 Games played a significant role in all ceremonies. A band was present in the Olympic Stadium at each event held there. Members of the official Olympic Band were paid due to the extensive time required in preparing and performing at the Games.

Most were professional musicians and the group was known as The Official Band of the Games of the Xth Olympiad. This group also performed on the radio and at various public events associated with the Games.

Three additional bands made up of college and high school students were used to augment the official band and to provide music at events held outside the Olympic Stadium. These groups were designated Band B, Band C (70 pieces each), and Band D (60 pieces). In addition to the professional band and three amateur groups, 30 bands totaling nearly 1,500 musicians performed at the Games as guest ensembles.

Trumpeters performed fanfares at the Marathon and opening, closing ceremonies, entertainment at the Olympic Village, and for other occasions during the Games.

The uniform of all Olympic musical organizations was totally white, with Continental caps and sashes in the Olympic colors of blue, yellow, black, green, and red. Members of the chorus wore berets and the Olympic rings were embroidered on all caps and berets.

Special arrangements of all the competing countries national anthem's were made in advance to match instrumentation of the American bands.

Based on a competitive selection process, the American composer, Bradley Keeler, was chosen to write a special Olympic Hymn for these Games

The music competition jury consisted of Ernest Schelling, Rubin Goldmark, Sigismund Stojowski, and Carl Engel, all from New York and A. Jurgelionis from Lithuania. Only Josef Suk's *Toward a New Life* received a prize and it was a silver in the Orchestra Division.

Maurice Eisner (music) and Jessica Lewis (lyrics) wrote a piece titled *Olympiad Welcome* for the 1932 Games.

Berlin/Garmisch-Partenkirchen (Winter, 1936) (Summer, 1936)

The Berlin Games of 1936 were the first to be shown on television with 25 large screens set up in theaters to permit locals to view the Games for free.

During the Vienna Congress of the IOC, the Olympic Hymn by Keeler (Los Angeles) was performed and offered to be recognized as the official Olympic Hymn of all time. The

German-American, Gustavus T. Kirby provided words for the tune. This motion was opposed by a Dr. Leward who felt it was common knowledge that Germany was recognized throughout the world as the principal home of music, and therefore, the German Committee for Organizing the Olympic Games would hold a competition for a text to a new Olympic Hymn composed by the German composer, Richard Strauss. Councillor Ihlert wrote the following in the Official Report of the 1936 Games about the Strauss hymn:

> *The composition, which is written in descending D major, begins with a treble-toned motif of the trumpets, this being thrice repeated and finding its echo in the hall, 'Olympia.' This motif is partly carried over by the instruments to the individual strophes and swells to a mighty volume at the conclusion. Fanfare-like themes by the brass and woodwind instruments introduce the chorus, which, rising above the stormy violin passages, hurls the invitation to the world, 'Welcome as our guests, ye Nations, Through our open gates draw nigh!' This maestoso theme in the first two measures brings the joyous excitement to the expression through the constant swelling and receding voices with ever-increasing intervals. The Olympia motif is intoned in the chorus for the first time at the end of the second strophe, being introduced by the brass instruments. The chorus, constituting a rhythmically closed unit and supported in its melody by the orchestra, developes in the course of further strophes to an impressive volume, the modulation technique which characterizes Strauss music being utilized here with excellent effect. Especially pronounced is the contrast in spirit as expressed in the fourth strophe, 'Praise on thee by deeds bestowing, Conquer well: Olympia!' through the light piano with only slight swellings and the elimination of the horns, which, however, return full strength and colour in the continuation of this strophe, 'Some will soon thy laurel carry, Crown of fame:Olympia!' Following a mighty orchestral crescendo, the composition reaches its climax in the twice repeated cry of joy, 'Olympia,' the full orchestra supporting the chorus throughout the principal motif in a rhythmical and melodious manner. With dithyrambic runs of the stringed instruments, fanfares of the trumpets and horns and a distant trumpet chorus the Hymn ends.*

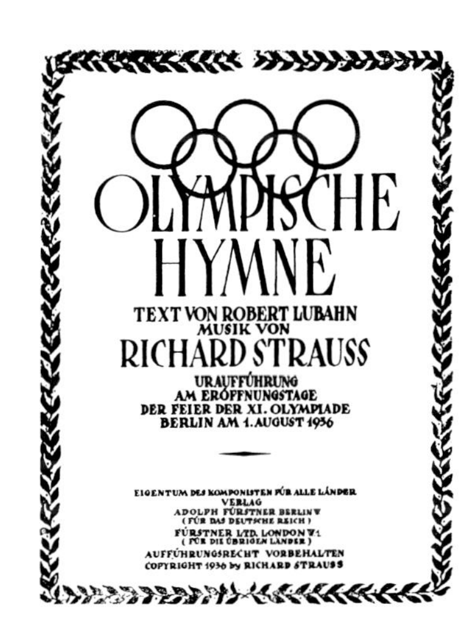

> *The Olympic Hymn is intended originally for large symphony orchestras with reinforced brass sections, while the rendition in the open air with an increased number of instruments, military music alone is recommended. The Hymn has also been arranged in C major for male choruses with small brass accompaniment as well as for a solo voice in C major with piano accompaniment, the composer himself being responsible for all of these arrangements."*

As a result of the competition to determine the text for this new hymn, prizes of 700, 200, and 100 reichmarks were awarded to Wilhelm von Scholz, Alfred von Kessel, and Gustav Franssen respectively. Due to the fact that the von Scholz text was suitable only for a German event and did not reflect the broader Olympic view, a new contest was announced and opened to all; not restricted to members of the Academy of Poets. This arrangement drew more than 3,000 manuscripts of which all but 50 were eliminated by Borries von Munchhausen (a ballad writer and member of the Academy of Poets). Of these 50 semifinalists, he chose four that he believed were suitable for the occasion. These were sent to Strauss for his final selection. Strauss then chose Robert Lubahn's work for the 100 reichmarks prize. After a long and laborious process of revisions, this finally became the text for the Strauss music and was completed during the winter of 1934–35.

After hearing this new work performed by a member of the Munich Opera, with Strauss himself playing the accompaniment during the Berlin Congress of 1935, the Executive Committee passed a motion that this work be recognized as the "Official Olympic Hymn for all time." A motion to this effect was passed by the entire Committee for Organizing the Olympic Games on July 30th, 1936. Strauss declined payment for the work and actually conducted the piece during the opening ceremonies.

The Reich Chamber of Music was instructed to make the appropriate arrangements for the musical needs of the Games. Due to the proud German musical heritage, it was decided that these musical offerings would be prominent in scope and quality. Each of the hymns of the various countries in attendance were arranged for chamber music, brass bands, and string orchestra. Special contacts were maintained with envoys of the competing countries during the rehearsals of the Berlin Philharmonic (conducted by Franz von Blon) so that a proper rendition of each work could be performed.

A special Olympic Concert was performed on August 15 at the Dietrich Eckart Open-Air Theater. This major event was attended by many in the German government, the Diplomatic Corps, State and Municipal Departments, Party Organizers, and foreign guests. Music that had been awarded the gold or silver medal in the musical competitions were performed and conducted by their composers. In addition, the Handel oratorio *Herakles*, was performed due to its explicit inner links with the Olympic ideal. It was estimated that 100,000 people attended the performances of the oratorio given on five different evenings between August 4 and 18. Expenses for the various musical events of the Games totaled more than 250,000 marks and included nearly 3,500 people.

Other music performed during the Games or at related Olympic functions included the *Andante cantabile* from Beethoven's *A Major Symphony* (at the Winter Games Opening Ceremonies), and Robert Schumann's *Assai agitato* (for the opening meeting of the IOC on July 29). During a session at the Pergamon Museum, Schein's *Pavane*, an Adagio from the *Hymn to Apollo* by Haydn, a dance suite from Handel (as performed by members of the Prussian State Theater), and the Chaconne from Gluck's *Paris and Helen* were all performed.

The Winter Games also saw the performance of several marches by a military band including: *Hellenmarsch*, *Yorkscher Marsch*, *Bayrischer Defiliermarsch*, *Fridericus Rex Marsch*, *Militarmarsch*, *RegimentsgruB*, *Kaiser Fredrich Marsch*, and *Koniggraber Siegesmarsch*. The Swedish National Anthem was played to end the ceremonies in Garmisch-Partenkirchen.

The Olympic film of the Berlin Games by Leni Riefenstahl includes music composed by Walter Gronostay and Herbert Windt. Windt also received the art prize for his radio music to accompany the original broadcast of the marathon.

The music jury in 1936 consisted of Professor Dr. Peter Raabe, Prasidialrat Hein Ihlert, professors Gustav Havenmann, Dr. Fritz Stein, Dr. Georg Schumann, Heinz Tiessen, and Max Trapp from Berlin as well as Yrjo Kilpinen, and Francesco Malipiero.

Breitkopf & Hartel of Leipzig published the official listing of national anthems for the 1936 Olympiad.

6

Post WWII

St. Moritz, Switzerland (Winter, 1948)

No musical records were preserved from the Winter Games in St. Moritz.

London, England (Summer, 1948)

The London Games of 1948 were the first held after the war and marked the first time Communist states sent athletes. It also marked the first time there were political defections at an Olympic Game.

Massed bands of the Brigade of Guards (200 members) played for the opening ceremonial March Past and stadium exit. During the March Past the group performed continuously for 45 minutes and was under the direction of Major G.H. Willcocks. It was reported that although the musicians were dressed in the ceremonial Bearskin and Tunic Order, not a single member passed out in the July heat. The massed bands alone performed the national anthem. A fanfare was played during the ceremonial release of the doves, symbolizing peace. The Olympic Hymn was performed followed by Handel's *Hallelujah Chorus* by massed bands and choirs. The Olympic Hymn previously composed in 1944 (these Games were canceled) by Roger Quilter with a setting of Rudyard Kipling's *Non Nobis Domine* was used here.

Sir Malcolm Sargent served as Director of Music and conducted the combined massed bands and choirs at the opening and closing ceremonies. There were 1,200 singers chosen for the large choir.

During the closing ceremonies words by Sir Alan Herbert, Chairman of the Literature Committee, were put to the famous tune *Londonderry Air* and performed by the large choir accompanied by the massed bands. Also included in the final events were the Trumpeters of the Household Calvary in ceremonial dress, who performed a fanfare in front of the Tribune just before the lowering of the Olympic Flag.

Gabriele Bianchi of Italy received a Bronze medal in the song category for his *Olympic Hymn*. In the instrumental composition category Canadian Jean Weinzweig won a Silver medal for the Divertimento for Flute and Streicher and Sergio Lauricella (Italy) won a bronze for *Toccata for Klavier*. The chorus and orchestra category saw three winners with the Gold medal going to Polish composer Zbrigniew Turski's *Olympijska Symphony*. The silver and bronze medals in this category went to Kalervo Tuukanen (Finland) for *Barenjagd for Orchestra* and Erling Brene (Denmark) for *Kraft for Orchestra* respectively. The music jury included Sir Arnold Pax, Edric Cundell, Sir George Dyson, Sir Stanley Marchant, and Sir Malcolm Sargent all from Britain, Paul Leroi from France, and Bruno Roghi from Italy.

The Summer Games of 1948 marked the last time for the arts competitions at the Olympic Games. This decision was made in 1949 by the IOC and was upheld in 1950 despite many protests. The IOC stated that the decision was made due to organizational and financial difficulties, the rule governing amateurism, and a lack of quality works.

There seems to be no interest in resurrecting these contests today, although the German Sports Museum at Cologne has been researching the project. This research will include an attempt to catalog a complete list of the approximately 4,000 or so works submitted in the competitions from 1912–1948.

Oslo, Norway (Winter, 1952)

Article 33 of the Olympic Charter specifies the procedure for the opening and closing ceremonies of the Games with Greece being the first to enter the stadium and the other participants to follow in alphabetical order by country. The host country, in this case Norway, entered last.

Due to the cold temperatures in Norway a military band and chorus could not be used outdoors and recorded music was used extensively. A special consultant compiled new gramophone recordings before the event and also created the programs for the ceremonies.

The Olympic Hymn from London was used here as well. This was the *Non nobis Domine*, music by Roger Quilter with words by Rudyard Kipling. The hymn was recorded by the Filharmonisk Selskaps Orkester and a large university choir (Kvinnelige Studenters Sangforening and Den Norske Studentersangforening) during the opening meeting in Oslo City Hall. A recording of this was played at the opening ceremonies in Bislett. The Norwegian National Anthem and the Royal Anthem were recorded by the Filharmonisk especially for the Games.

The Olympic Fanfare (Signal Theme) was an adaptation of a short piece written for the World Ski Championships in 1940 by Norwegian Johannes Hanssen. The 1940 Winter Games were canceled due to the war and the piece was not used until this time. It was based on the old folk song *Mass og han Lasse* and proved to be quite popular. Although an old recording of this remained in the files of the Norwegian Broadcasting Corporation, the composer recorded a new version with the wind players of the Filharmonisk Selskaps Orkester and the Radio Orchestra.

The theme was used extensively throughout the 1952 Games and was recorded with a welcome greeting in Norwegian and English from the President of the Winter Games to the guests of the city of Oslo. Another recording was made by Hampus Huldt Nystrom, performed by Den Norske Studentersangforening with Alfred Maurstad as soloist and Sigurd Torkildsen conducting, that included the entire folk song.

In the Winter Games of 1952, 30 nations participated.

The opening ceremonies of these Games had to be altered due to the sudden death of H.M. King George VI on February 6. Music played for most events was of a more solemn nature, yet marches were still played as the athletes entered the stadium and the signal theme was used for the entrance of the torch.

Helsinski, Finland (Summer, 1952)

These were the first Games in which USSR athletes participated.

A five minute fanfare was composed for the 1940 Olympic Games by Aarre Merikanto. Since those Games were canceled, the Committee for Organizing the Olympic Games requested that he shorten a version of this fanfare to about two minutes so it could be used in 1952. The piece was then adopted as the official fanfare of the XV Olympiad. The Finnish Broadcasting Corporation requested that an even shorter version (20–30 seconds) be arranged to herald the Olympic Broadcasts. This shorter version was used at all victory celebrations in the various arenas.

At the 1950 IOC Congress in Copenhagen, it was declared once again that there was no official Olympic Hymn. New host Organizing Committees of the Games were granted the right to use the hymn composed by Richard Strauss (1936) or the one by Roger Quilter (1948) that had been sung in London. They were also given the opportunity to commission a hymn of their own. Based on this IOC decision, the Finnish Committee for Organizing the Olympic Games decided to host a competition for both a new set of text and a new melody.

The competition for a new verse was concluded on September 30, 1951 and first prize was awarded to Niilo Partanen with second and third awards going to Toivo Lyy and Heikki Asunta respectively. The judging panel consisted of Professor Lauri Viljanen, Mr. Jarl Louhija, and Mr. Arno Tuurna. Lyy also wrote a shortened version of his words after receiving permission from the panel.

The selection panel then permitted the music competitors to choose any of the three verse prize winners for their music. The musical competition opened on October 17, 1951 and closed on January 31, 1952. The adjudication panel consisted of composers Jouko Tolonen, Tanelo Kuusisto, Professor Bengt Carlsson, and Mr. Arno Tuurna. The only prize awarded went to elementary teacher, Jaakko Linjama. Mr. Linjama's music was set to the words of Toivo Lyy. This hymn was sung at the opening ceremonies on July 3, and at the closing ceremonies on July 19, 1952.

The new Olympic Hymn and a cantata by Taneli Kuusisto (*A Finnish Prayer*) was performed by a competitively selected 526 member mixed chorus. Mr. Martti Turunen was selected as the director. Limited rehearsals were held and the full group practiced for the first time at Messuhalli II and at the Stadium two days before the Games. A full dress rehearsal was held with the band on July 18. The 310 female members of the chorus wore Finnish national costumes and the 216 men wore white shirts and dark trousers. All members received a commemorative medal as a memento. A breakdown of the number of voices on each part follows: first soprano–97, second soprano–74, first alto–64, second alto–75, first tenor–45, second tenor–42, first bass–59, and second bass–70.

The massed bands of the Finnish Army were used to fulfill the ceremonial functions for the Games. Musicians were provided from seven different garrison bands and the Army Schools of Music. The conductor of the groups was Chief Bandmaster Martti Parantainen, who had seven assistants performing various functions. In total, 180 band members were used throughout the course of the Games.

Garrison bands practiced the music in advance at their respective locations and met during joint rehearsals in Helsinki just before the beginning of the Games. The full complement of musicians was used at the opening and closing ceremonies with the group broken down into smaller units for the various functions. At victory ceremonies a 120-piece ensemble was utilized.

The bands for the Games were required to perform at the following functions: opening and closing ceremonies (including the Olympic Hymn with choir, Olympic Fanfare, national anthems, and march music during the entrance and exit of the teams), provide music for the competitions (Olympic Fanfare, the victor's national anthem, and various light music), provide march music for the gymnastic exhibitions and the national anthems at the Olympic villages as the teams national flags were raised and lowered.

Military band scores for the various national anthems were secured well in advance. Countries were also asked to send gramophone recordings so that the conductors could become familiar with the tunes before the Games began. Band members wrote out arrangements of the hymn from the scores provided.

The massed band was placed at the north end of the stadium below the new electrical scoreboard. Mr. Turunen conducted the combined bands and choirs. During the opening ceremonies, the band played 24 marches nonstop. This medley lasted nearly an hour.

The famous Finnish composer, Jean Sibelius, prepared a march arrangement of his *Song of the Athenians* which was used at the closing ceremonies as the flag of the nations exited the stadium. This arrangement was not commissioned by the Committee for Organizing the Olympic Games but was provided by the composer based on his personal initiative during the course of the Games.

Cortina D'Ampezzo, Italy (Winter, 1956)

The new official Olympic Hymn composed by Michal Spisak opened the 1956 Games in Cortina D'Ampezzo, Italy. For the March Past, an original musical selection was composed by Giuseppe Blanc of Turin (best known for his waltz *Malombra*). This new work was titled *Olympic Parade*. Blanc also composed special fanfares for the prize ceremonies.

The herald's costumes were made by the wardrobe department at La Scala based on actual Renaissance patterns.

Melbourne, Australia (Summer, 1956)

An Australian quarantine law caused the equestrian events to be held in Stockholm. These Games were marked by the first major boycotts by regularly participating countries. In protest of Israel's takeover of the Suez Canal, Egypt, Iraq, and Lebanon withdrew. Holland, Spain, and Switzerland did not send teams to protest the Soviet invasion of Hungary.

Prior to the Games in Melbourne an international competition was held by the IOC to once again create a new Olympic Hymn. The words were prescribed by the IOC and were extracts from the works of the Greek poet, Pindar who had been commissioned to write ceremonial hymns to honor the victors of the ancient Olympic Games. A commemorative medal and $1,000 (US) were offered as prizes. The money was provided by Prince Peirre of Monaco. A total of 387 compositions from 40 countries were entered, including six from the host country. The winner was Michal Spisak, a Polish composer living in Paris. The new hymn was presented three times; at the opening and closing ceremonies, and at the opening of the IOC Congress.

Several local ethnic groups performed folk songs and dancing entertainment for the athletes. No names are available as these were unofficial events and not carefully documented.

There were two anthems played for the Australian gold medal winner in these Games. For a long time the Australian National Anthem was *God Save the Queen*. However, for several decades it had been popular to play *Advance Australia Fair* at special events. The uncertainty reached a climax at the Melbourne Games when Australian Shirley Strickland won the 80 meter hurdles. Both anthems were played for her while she was on the winner's dais. She recalled that this double-anthem episode was one of the most pleasant experiences of her athletic career.

In December of 1954, all nations were asked to supply the Organizing Committee with the music of their national anthem scored for military band so that there would be no doubt as to the correct anthem for any particular nation. An additional letter was sent in August, 1955 to those nations who had accepted invitations and had not yet supplied their anthem.

At the 1955 IOC meeting it was decided that no national anthem should last more than one minute and it was necessary to abbreviate all the anthems provided. This was done by Squadron Leader L.H. Hicks, Director of Music of the Royal Australian Air Force. To reduce the anthem length to within the specified playing time, some sections were omitted to ensure closing on an acceptable cadence. *God Save the Queen* and *The Star Spangled Banne*r were easily arranged because shortened versions were commonly used. Some lengthy anthems had their main sections cut so that the final closing bars would be included. In the case of the rather long anthem of the former Soviet Union, which had several differing verses, the best arrangement under one minute was selected .

All anthems were scored for full military band, copies of which were made for bands playing at outdoor ceremonies. Tape recordings were made by the Central Band of the Royal Australian Air Force and sent to the Organizing Committee which had discs made for use at the outdoor venues. The entire process of preparing the selections took six months.

Scores of the national anthem's are now in the archives of the Central Band, Royal Australian Air Force, Laverton, Victoria. The master copies of the recordings are in the possession of Amalgamated Wireless Australia Ltd.

At the suggestion of a 17-year-old Chinese boy, the athletes marched together for the closing ceremonies instead of by country as a show of world unity.

Stockholm, Sweden (Summer, 1956)

As mentioned earlier, equestrian events of the 1956 Games were moved to Stockholm due to concerns about importing disease in Australia. When the King declared these Games open, fanfares were sounded from the two stadium towers, just as in 1912. These fanfares were from

Kungarop from the *Marcia Carolus Rex*, a Swedish calvary march composed in the 1800's. Bertil Driving was the conductor of the trumpet groups which were formed from the Royal Swedish Navy. Michal Spisak's *Olympic Hymn* was used as the official hymn and was sung during the ceremonies by members of the Stockholm Choral Union as conducted by Hilding Asker. Accompanying the chorus were members of the combined bands: the Royal Vdastmanland, the Royal Svea, and the Royal Sidermanland Air Force Wings, conducted by Rertif Wiklander.

Squaw Valley, California, USA (Winter, 1960)

Walt Disney was the chair of the Squaw Valley Games Pageantry Committee. Charles A. Hirt was the music coordinator. The committee was supported by the Music Educators National Conference (Dr. Karl Ernst, President and Vanett Lawler, Executive Secretary), and the California Music Educators, (Dr. Joseph Landon, President).

The opening ceremonies were well coordinated and worthy of a true "Disney" event. The flag raising ceremony included music with fireworks and was followed by a parade to *The Parade of the Olympians*. A massed band and chorus accompanied the singing of the Olympic Hymn. Robert Linn arranged *The Olympic Hymn* from the original by Samaras, with the English translation by Basil Swift. During the torch transfer *Conquest* was played by the massed bands. *God of Our Fathers* was played by the massed group during a religious ceremony narrated by Karl Malden. After the Olympic Oath they played the United States National Anthem. The group then played the *Parade of the Olympians* once again as 20,000 balloons were released during the recessional (accompanied by fireworks).

The United States Marine Band, Washington, D.C., directed by Lieutenant Colonel Albert Schoepper, was the official band of the Games and performed at all Olympic ceremonies. Musicians from 52 California and Nevada high schools, totaling 1,285 instrumentalists and 2,645 vocalists, also participated in various ceremonies. The massed student bands were under the direction of Clarence Sawhill from the University of California, Los Angeles (UCLA), and Dr. Charles Hirt from the University of Southern California (USC), directed the massed choirs.

The United States Marine Band played for all gold medal ceremonies. A fifteen-minute carillon and fanfare was played from loud speakers throughout the valley and high in the mountains before each day's ceremonies. The Marine Band played the gold medalist's national anthem, followed by *Parade of the Olympians*.

The estimated attendance was 250,000 for the Squaw Valley Winter Games.

The closing ceremonies again used *Parade of the Olympians* as the athletes entered the stadium. The Greek and United States National Anthems were played as the flags were raised followed by the Austrian Anthem (site of the 1964 Winter Games). Following a brief address by IOC president, Avery Brundage, the Olympic Hymn was played as the Olympic Flag was lowered. During the carrying of the flag horizontally by the eight-member Olympic Honor Guard, the band played *Ode Triumphant*. The ceremonies concluded with a performance of *No Man is An Island,* another balloon launch, and finally *Parade of the Olympians* as the athletes left the arena.

Listed below are the high school bands and choirs from California and Nevada that participated in the ceremonies.

California Bands
Berkeley
Ceres
El Camino Eagle
Escondido Union
Harry Ells
Hollywood
Placer
Porterville Union
Roosevelt
Sonora Union
St. Helena
Thomas Downey

California Choirs
Abraham Lincoln
Acalanes
Antioch
Bellflower
Berkeley
Central Union
Dinuba
Hillsdale
Hollywood
Hughson Union
Huntington Park
Live Oak Union
Madera
Modesto
Mt. Diablo
Nevada Union
Oakland
Placer
Porterville Union
Red Bluff
Reedley
San Juan
Sanger Union
Santa Rosa
Sonora Union
South Fork
South Gate
Tamalpais
Thomas Downey
Vallejo
Watersonville
Willow Glen

Nevada Bands
Carson
Churchill County
Elko
Humbolt County
Mineral County
Reno

Nevada Choirs
Carson
Elko and Reno

Rome, Italy (Summer, 1960)

South Africa was barred from these Games to protest its racial policies. In the past, only those countries on the losing side of a world war had been barred.

After failing to find a new hymn for the 1960 Games in Rome the IOC decided to name the hymn from the first Olympic Games in Athens (1896), with music by Spiros Samaras and text by Kostis Palamas, as the permanent Olympic Hymn. For these games the hymn was translated into Italian by Sigfrido Troilo. Performances at the ceremonies were directed by Maestro Bonaventura Somma with help from Domenico Fantini, Conductor of the Carabinieri Band, Alterto Di Miniello, Conductor of the Italian Air Force Band, Antonio Fuselli, Conductor of the Public Service Police Band, Giovanni D'Angelo, Vice Conductor of the Band of the Finance Guards, and Olivio Di Domenico, Conductor of the Band of the Finance Guards.

The first four bars of *Hymn of the Sun* from Mascagni's opera, *Iris,* was used as the fanfare leit-motif heard at every official ceremony during the Games. Recordings of all national anthems, marches needed during various ceremonies, and other musical selections were prepared in advance of the Games by the above mentioned conductors.

There were six different bands (four military groups of 100 each and two civil groups of about 60) used at various times during the Games. Each band received 24–25 musical scores to cover their respective needs, including ten copies of each national anthem. In addition to these bands, the Band of the Tram and Bus Corporation (conducted by Maestro Alu), and the Naples Band of the Italian Navy were utilized as needed.

Recordings of the national anthems were made at the studios of the Italian Radio and Television (RAI) by the four military bands. These recordings were designed to be used at awards ceremonies when one of the bands could not be present in the event of anticipated traffic problems. There was great concern that movement of bands from one event to another would be very difficult given the usual traffic congestion in Rome. Fortunately, this provision was not necessary, as the bands always arrived in time.

During the opening ceremonies, only the Carabinieri Band accompanied by the Choir of the National Academy of Santa Cecilia, performed the Olympic Hymn and Italian National Anthem. To alleviate problems of fatigue, the four bands played alternately during the opening ceremony March Past (43 minutes) and recessional (41 minutes). At these ceremonies, twelve marches lasting 3–4 minutes each were used.

Innsbruck, Austria (Winter, 1964)

The technical director of the Vienna Folk Opera, Professor Walter von Hosslin, played a prominent role in planning the opening ceremonies. Joseph Scmiedhuber performed the national anthem and marches played included *Paradedefiliermarsch* by Ambrosch, *Olympiamarsch* by Labsky, *Schonfeldmarsch* by Ziehrer, *47th Regiment March* by Wagner, *Salute to Luxemburg* by Pazke, *Frisch* by Pesch, *Rechts-schaut March* by Tanzer, *3rd Regiment's March* by Schneider, and *O du mein Osterreich* by Preiss. Other music during the ceremonies included festival music by Karl Piliss. Trumpets and trombones were used for the Olympic Fanfare and Hymn. Additional celebration music by Viktor Hruby was performed and church bells rang out to signal the end of the opening ceremonies as the Olympic Flame was lit.

During the closing ceremonies several musical groups performed including a 100-member male chorus with 16 trumpets and two trombones.

Tokyo, Japan (Summer, 1964)

The Tokyo Committee for Organizing the Olympic Games convened two subcommittees to oversee the Fine Arts Exhibition and special performances for the XVIII Olympiad of 1964. It was decided that there would be ten displays—four in fine arts and six in performance. The performances were held in the Kabukiza Theater, Toranomon Hall (in the Imperial Household Agency), Shimbashi Embujo, Tokyo Bunka Kaikan—Ueno Park, Geijutsuza Theater, and Kanze Kaikan—Omagari.

A wide variety of music was performed at the opening ceremonies. As the athletes entered the stadium a medley of marches was performed that included:

Olympic March, Y. Koseki
Old Comrades and *Zeppelin*, Karl Teike
On the Quarter Deck, K.J. Alford
Hands Across the Sea and *El Capítan*, John Philip Sousa
Sambre et Meuse, Planquette
Celebration March, I. Dan
Sabre and Spear, H. Starke
Our Director, F.E. Bigelow
March Regiment, Morney
Bravura, C.E. Duble

Auld Lang Syne, with new words, was performed at the closing ceremonies as well as the traditional playing of the Greek, Japanese, and Mexican National Anthems.

The decision in 1958 to use *The Olympic Hymn* by Spiros Samaras (1896) as the official Olympic Hymn for all future Games remained firm here and at every Olympic Game that followed.

GRENOBLE, FRANCE (WINTER, 1968)

The 1968 Winter Games marked the first time that ABC Sports used the familiar *Bugler's Dream* of Leo Arnaud as their television coverage musical trademark. This fanfare was also used by ABC for their Wide World of Sports program for a number of years and continues to find its way into television coverage.

Leo Arnaud was born on July 24, 1904 and studied music at the Lyon and Paris Conservatories. His composition teachers included Vincent D'Indy and Maurice Ravél. Although he graduated from the French Academy as a trombonist, he also became proficient in percussion, trumpet, french horn, cello, and saxophone. It has been reported that Ravél often relied on Arnaud to test possible trombone parts for his famous *Bolero.* He immigrated to the United States in 1931 and became the drummer for Fred Waring's The Pennsylvanians.

Arnaud also spent some time composing film scores and is credited with the music for Dr. Zhivago and Voyage of the Damned. *Olympic Fanfare, La Chase,* and his *Bugler's Dream* were actually part of a larger work composed in 1954. Arnaud died on April 26, 1991 in Hamptonville, North Carolina.

The Olympic Music Hall was established in the center of Innsbruck and hosted such greats as Ella Fitzgerald, Gilbert Bécaud, Charles Aznavour, Manitas de Plata, and Johnny Halliday. In ten days 20,000 paying guests attended concerts by these performers.

Ten additional concerts were held in Grenoble during the month of February at the Municipal Theater, and the Cultural Center. They included Giorgy Cziffra, the National Orchestra of Paris conducted by Charles Munch and Serge Baudo, and the University Choir with a lecture by Olivier Messiaen. Other artists included Lili Lastine, Felicien Wolff, and Marie-Claire Alain.

Chant Olympic by Francis Lai was sung by the French singer Mireille Mathieu.

Mexico City, Mexico (Summer, 1968)

One of the most controversial events of the 1968 Games was the Black Power protests of the United States runners.

A 40-piece trumpet fanfare followed by the playing of the Mexican National Anthem marked the opening of the XIX Olympiad in Mexico City. A 300-piece band provided the music for the March Past and entrance into the stadium. *Sakura* was played as the Olympic Flag was brought into the stadium and during the release of 40,000 balloons *La Zandunga*, a traditional Mexican song, was played.

Ancient Mexican music on drums and reed flutes accompanied a haunting call played by a giant conch to announce the arrival of the Olympic Torch.

During the closing ceremonies the theme from the finale to Beethoven's *Symphony No. 9* was played to signify the transition to the Munich Games in 1972. This was followed by 1,000 mariachis playing *La Negra*, *Guadalajara*, and the traditional Mexican song of farewell, *Las Golondrinas*. The festive atmosphere continued well into the night, spilling into the nearby streets of the city after the official ending of the Games.

SAPPORO, JAPAN (WINTER, 1972)

Article 58 of the Olympic Charter specifies that the winning athlete's national anthem be played at the awarding of medals for each event. At the 1972 Sapporo Games, Canada, the Democratic People's Republic of Korea, the German Democratic Republic, and Germany all had different national anthem's since the previous Japanese Games in Tokyo. This made it necessary for new versions of their countries anthem to be submitted. Rearranging the anthems to fit the one minute time limit was done by Yosaku Suma.

A special fanfare was composed for the Games by Akira Miyoshi and titled *Fanfare of the Sapporo Winter Games*.

Additional music composed for the Games included:

Music Honoring H.I.M. The Emperor, Osamu Shimzu
Sapporo Olympic March, Naozumi Yamamoto
The Land of Glorious Snow, Minoru Shimizu
The Rainbow and Snow, Saburo Iwakawa
Music for the Olympic Flag Transfer Ceremony , Yuji Koseki
Skater's Waltz, Yuji Koseki
Hymn for the opening ceremony, Shuntaro Tanigawa
Hymn for the closing ceremony, Minoru Miki
Farewell Song, Yoshinao Nakada

The Cultural Program included performances of traditional Kabuki and Noh drama. The Snow Festival provided an excellent showcase for the fine arts. It included a guest performance by the Munich Philharmonic Orchestra which was the first half of an exchange with the NHK Symphony (Japan), who later performed at the Munich Games. Also performing was the Sapporo Symphony Orchestra.

Munich, Germany (Summer, 1972)

Probably the greatest tragedy of any Olympic Games was in Munich where eleven Israeli athletes and coaches were killed by eight Palestinian terrorists. The Games were suspended for 34 hours, but continued in a greatly subdued atmosphere.

Karl Orff created a four act opera called *Gruss der Jugend* (*Greeting to Youth* or *Youth Salute*) for the opening of these Games. It is an arrangement of the old English canon *Rota*.

The music for the parade of nations was composed by band leader, Kurt Edelhagen. The medley was designed to change its character with each different group of athletes who entered the stadium. Additional musical selections were composed and arranged by Peter Herbolzheimer, Dieter Reith, and Jerry van Rooyen.

The Neubiberg Armed Forces Orchestra conducted by Captain Ronals Linter performed the *Olympic Fanfare* composed by Herbert Rehbein. This piece was selected during an open competition for a new fanfare. During these Games *The Olympic Hymn* by Samaras was arranged by Alfred Goodman and performed at the stadium by the Bavarian Rundfunk, conducted by Willi Matthes.

Music for the arrival of the Olympic Flame was composed by Wilhelm Killmayer and was also played by the Bavarian Rundfunk with accompaniment by brass soloists placed in various places throughout the Stadium. *Ekecheirija* by Krysztof Penderecke for speaker, chorus, soloist, and electronic music was performed following the Olympic Pledge. It was composed to represent an Olympic oracle of the god Apollo.

Innsbruck, Austria (Winter, 1976)

There were four bands and a chorus of 200 children that helped with the opening ceremonies at Innsbruck in 1976. The Tyrolean Military Band played at all victory ceremonies. The Wiltener, a traditional band based in Innsbruck and directed by Professor Sepp Tanzer, performed at the closing ceremonies.

The Olympic Ball was the social highlight of the Innsbruck Games. Those in attendance were entertained by the Max Gregory Orchestra with special guest Peter Ustinov.

Montréal, Canada (Summer, 1976)

Many African nations (including Tanzania, Iraq, and Guyana) boycotted the Montréal Games in protest of the New Zealand rugby team traveling to South Africa.

The music for the Montréal Games was designed around a common theme and was constructed similar to a movie sound track. Moods and emotions were carefully considered and special attention was given to the television audience perspective at all times. For this reason neo-romantic compositional style was desired. Although Canadian composer André Mathieu had died in 1968, the committee decided a variety of his works would lend themselves to the Olympic atmosphere and could be arranged in the short time available. By extracting musical themes from his works, a link could be provided for transitions in ceremonies, the Olympic Fanfare, songs of welcome and farewell, as well as the cantata used in the opening ceremonies. Victor Vogel, a native of Montréal, was selected to orchestrate and arrange Mathieu's music and coordinate the overall musical score for the Games. Art Philips assisted Mr. Vogel in this huge undertaking.

André Mathieu died in 1968 at the age of 39. He was a child prodigy and had received a government scholarship to study music at the age of seven. Mathieu is credited with composing as early as the age of four. During his short lifetime he toured extensively and won first prize in 1942 at the International Competition for Young Composers for his *Concertino for Piano and Orchestra No. 2, Opus 13*. He performed this work with the New York Philharmonic when he was 13. Mathieu is credited with more than 100 compositions, most in the symphonic and piano concerto genre.

A fanfare of royal trumpets opened the 1976 Games in Montréal. *O Canada* was played by a youth orchestra comprised of musicians from 30 countries representing all five continents. The Olympic Orchestra directed by Victor Vogel performed *March of the Athletes* for the processional. This piece was a symphonic suite composed of neo-romantic themes by Mathieu. Following tradition, the Olympic Flag was brought into the stadium to the strains of Samaras' *The Olympic Hymn*. The march *Bayrischer Defilir* and the *Stern* polka accompanied the Munich delegation dressed in folk costumes as a prelude to the transfer of the flag from

Munich to Montréal. The Montréal Dancers performed a suite of Quebec music in front of the Queen including *Danse de la plongeuse, Auprès de ma blonde, Marianne s'en va-t-au moulin, Danse des ceintures* and *Reel des cinq jumelles*. The flame was brought into the stadium during the Olympic Fanfare. The Olympic Orchestra and Choir (comprised of members of the choirs of the *Petits Chanteurs du mont Royal*, the *Disciples de Massenet*, and singers from the *Union des artistes de Montréal)* performed during the lighting of the flame. A special cantata was written by Louis Chantigny especially for the 1976 Games and was inspired from Mathieu's *Romantic Rhapsody for Piano and Orchestra.*

A highlight of the opening ceremonies was a seven-minute ballet performed by student gymnasts from several different countries and again accompanied by Mathieu's *Concerto No. 3*, *The Quebec*.

The closing ceremonies followed what by then had become very strict protocol. The Olympic Fanfare was sounded and there was a short ballet of school children. The *Parade of the Athletes* was played by the orchestra, and a symphonic suite of traditional Amerindian music played on traditional instruments (tom-toms, rattles, and bells) ushered in the athletes. Near the end of the parade Mathieu's *Danse sauvage* was performed, bringing the procession to a close. The Soviet National Anthem was played as their flag was raised in tribute to the next Games scheduled for Moscow.

The Orpheus choir sang Samaras' *The Olympic Hymn* a cappella as the Olympic Flag was lowered. The flag was removed from the stadium to drum rolls and the combined choir and orchestra. The music for this was taken from Mathieu's symphonic poem, *Mistassini*. During the extinguishing of the flame, Montréal jazz musician Maynard Ferguson performed a trumpet solo.

As a preview to the Moscow Games there was a live broadcast from the USSR on the stadium screens of a choir singing *Kalinka*. The evening ended with the athletes, Amerindians and young girls dancing the *Farandole*.

There was a live ensemble present in the stadium during all events in case there were technical difficulties with the prepared recorded music. A 50-minute recording of the music from the Montréal Games was also made available to the general public. The Committee for Organizing the Olympic Games published an English and French version of the song *Welcome to Montréal,* sung by René Simard, one year before the Games. Simard had won the first Frank Sinatra award and an international song competition in Tokyo during 1974. Signature tunes were also included on these recordings for radio and television promotional purposes.

White Rock by Rick Wakeman was used as a musical background for the documentary film of the 1976 Winter Games in Montréal.

Lake Placid, New York, USA (Winter, 1980)

At Lake Placid an effort was made to call attention to the deeper meaning of the Olympics—namely the development of the whole person. The Olympic Arts Festival was one of the largest ever held in the United States. Caroline Hopkins, founder of the Syracuse Symphony, chaired the Fine Arts Committee. Violinist Yehudi Menuhin was honorary co-chair and Edward Villella, former principal dancer with the New York City Ballet, was honorary vice-chair.

More than $1,000,000 was raised for the festival. Funding came from the Lake Placid Committee for Organizing the Olympic Games, the Heritage Trust of Parks and Recreation of New York State Council on the Arts, The National Endowment for the Arts, private individuals, foundations, corporations, and marketing contracts.

There were two films produced on the XIII Winter Olympics. The first, *Olympic Overture*, featured Menuhin and the Cantilena Chamber Players. It was aired on PBS and served as the official announcement of the opening of the National Fine Arts Program for the Games. The Cantalina Chamber Players new work *Round a Common Center* composed by Lucas Foss and based on the poem *The Runner* by W.H. Auden, was also a part of the premiere telecast on February 10, 1980. The second film was a documentary on how the artists and athletes contributed to the success of the event.

Mrs. Nettie Marie Jones funded the publication of a 70-page brochure titled Art at the

Olympics. A greater number of new artistic works were commissioned for these Games than at any other arts festival held in the United States. A new chamber symphony, titled *Kinesis* and composed by William Conti for the Los Angeles Symphony, was performed for the first time at the Games.

A major jazz composition, *Jazzmobile,* was also premiered at Lake Placid. Billy Taylor was the artistic director and Frank Foster was the composer and director.

There were three traditional American music compositions premiered at these Games. They included *Snow Blind* for hammered dulcimer, fiddle, and bass by Walt Michael; *The Man in the Middle* for vocals, guitar, fiddle, and bass, by Tom "Harley" Campbell; and *Whiteface Reel* a fiddle tune with guitar and bass accompaniment by Tom McReesh. In addition, the St. Regis String Band, Robin Schade and the North Country Minstrel, the Green Grass Cloggers (traditional dance ensemble from North Carolina), and the Barbershoppers and Sweet Adelines from throughout upstate New York all made appearances. The SUNY, Plattsburgh's resident chamber ensemble, also performed.

International performers who were involved throughout the Games included Dionne Warwick, Jamie Farr, Tanya Tucker, Dr. Hook, Harry Chapin, Vantage Point, and The Nighthawks. Most of the funds raised were for commissioning new works and paying performer's expenses. Therefore, a variety of existing local facilities were used instead of constructing new ones.

In association with the Games, the New York State Education Department held a composition contest won by three Penfield High School students.

Although the arts festival was a huge success by most standards, the organizers were not satisfied. This was due in part to limited television coverage and also to what some believed was a lack of status conferred by the Lake Placid Committee for Organizing the Olympic Games, which was responsible for the overall structure of the Games.

Moscow, USSR (Summer, 1980)

In protest of the Soviet invasion of Afghanistan, the United States led a major western nation boycott of the 1980 Moscow Games. Despite this, the Games proceeded with much pomp and polish.

Soviet culture and life were an important highlight of the 1980 Games in Moscow. Attention was given to the protocol needed to adhere to strict Olympic regulations and the overall pageant aspect of the Games. The actual scenarios were approved well in advance of the Games in June of 1979 by both the Organizing Committee Presidium and the IOC Executive Board.

Professor Joseph Tumanov, People's Artist of the USSR, set up the production and direction group. He was aided by Assistant Professor B.N. Petrov. Chief Conductor was Odissei Dimitriadi with Mikhail Godenko in charge of the ballet productions. The chief choirmaster was Vladislav Sokolov and Raphael Kazachek the chief artist.

The Kremlin chimes were heard over a system of loud speakers to signal the beginning of the opening ceremonies on July 19, 1980. The *Festive Overture* by Dimitri Shostakovich was designated as the official theme song of the Games and was performed to announce the start of the ceremonies. After words of encouragement by IOC President Lord Killanin and the Committee for Organizing the Olympic Games President Ignati Novikov, Soviet President Leonid Brezhnev declared the XXII Games open. This was followed by the playing of *The Olympic Hymn* as the Olympic Flag was presented and raised. The flame was ignited as the *Ode to Sport*, written by Soviet composer Eduard Artemyev was played. The Soviet Anthem signaled the ending of the official opening ceremonies. Following these events the artistic and sports program began showcasing various displays of athletes and dancers.

The closing ceremonies took place on August 3. The athletes entered the stadium track to the strain of a march. Of special note were the remarks of outgoing president of the IOC, Lord Killanin who spoke of the special spirit of the Games and his regrets for those athletes who did not participate (a reference to the teams from the West who boycotted the event).

Once again the Olympic Flag was lowered to the strains of *The Olympic Hymn* and was followed by the cantata, *Ode to Sport.* A mixed brass band played and marched as girls came out on to the field and performed exercises with hoops and ribbons. As part of the farewell ceremonies, the song *Goodbye Moscow* written by Alexandra Pakhmutova with words by Nikolai Dobronravov, was played as the giant Misha (the bear-like mascot of the Games) balloon floated toward the sky.

Los Angeles, California, USA (Winter, 1984)

The Eastern Block countries countered the 1980 boycott of the Moscow Games with one of their own in Los Angeles.

Popular music such as Diana Ross' *Reach Out and Touch (Somebody's Hand)* and Lionel Richie's *All Night Long,* as well as Gershwin's *Rhapsody in Blue,* played a big part in the ceremonies at the 1984 Games.

John Williams' *Fanfare Olympique* (Olympic Fanfare and Theme) was the official theme of the Games and was played at all ceremonies. Marvin Hamlisch wrote an original song, *Welcome* (with lyrics by Dean Pitchford) which was performed by the 1,039-voice Olympic Choir. Dr. Charles C. Hirt served as the choir director.

Special music was highlighted in the opening ceremonies. The musical/visual extravaganza was titled **The Music of America** and was divided into six segments depicting different aspects of American culture.

The American Suite included Copeland's *Fanfare for the Common Man*, *Strike up the Band* by George Gershwin, and an American medley arranged by Earl Brown and Tony Fox.

The Pioneer Spirit featured *How the West was Won* by Alfred Newman and *Rodeo and Hoedown* also by Aaron Copeland.

Dixieland Jamboree included *Waiting for the Robert E. Lee*, music by Lewis Muir and lyrics by Wolfe Gilbert; *Way Down Yonder in New Orleans*, music by Turner Layton and lyrics by Henry Creamer; and the traditional *Basin Street Blues* and *When the Saints Go Marching In*. Also in this segment were several gospel songs performed by the 300-voice Olympic Gospel Choir and Olympic Band (the largest ever established for such an event) led by Arthur Bartner of University of Southern California.

Urban Rhapsody included *Rhapsody in Blue* by Gershwin, *Manhattan* with music by Richard Rogers and lyrics by Lorenz Hart, and *I Got Rhythm* also by Gershwin. *Rhapsody in Blue* was performed by 84 pianists dressed in white, each sitting at their own white grand piano.

The World is a Stage was divided into three sets.

Astaire and Rogers was punctuated with Irving Berlin's *Let's Face the Music and Dance* and *Cheek to Cheek.*

Big Band Swing session that included *It Don't Mean a Thing If It Ain't Got That Swing* by Ellington and Mills, *Moonlight Serenade* by Glenn Miller and Mitchell Parish, *In the Mood* by Joe Garland, *I'm Getting Sentimental Over You* by George Bassman and Ned Washington, *Opus No. 1* by Sy Oliver, *One O'clock Jump* by Count Basie, and *Sing, Sing, Sing* by Louis Prima. The highlight on the stadium field for this set was the jitterbug performed by 300 Jazzercise instructors from all over the United States.

That's Entertainment and began with *Singin' in the Rain* by Brown and Freed. This was followed by *America* from Bernstein's West Side Story, *One* from Marvin Hamlisch and Edward Kleban's A Chorus Line, *Fame* from the musical by the same name (music by Gore and lyrics by Pitchford), and lastly *Beat It* by Michael Jackson. Dancers in this segment included 1,500 members of the Olympic Dance Corps and Olympic Drill Teams.

Finale included more music from *One,* followed by *America the Beautiful* by Samuel A. Ward with lyrics by Katherine Lee Bates.

The athletes entered the stadium to a medley of tunes from around the world. This was followed by the traditional addresses to the audience and the flag raising ceremony conducted while *The Olympic Hymn* by Samaras was played. The music used for the torch lighting ceremony (*Olympian)* was written by Philip Glass. In preparation for the Olympic Oath, Alfred Newman's march *Conquest* was played. It was followed by Beethoven's *Ode to Joy* and *Reach Out and Touch (Somebody's Hand)* by Valerie Simpson and Nicholas Ashford, with lyrics written especially for the 1984 Games. The entire crowd joined in singing this song as the athletes left the stadium.

Others involved with the opening ceremonies included Dr. Bill Moffit who served as director of the Fanfare Trumpets, Captain David Deitrick who directed the United States Army Herald Trumpets, the Holman United Methodist Church Choir, Gwen Wyatt, director, the Second Baptist Church of Los Angeles, Dr. J. Harrison Wilson, director of the Aman Folk Ensemble, and the International Childrens Choir.

The All-American Band used at the Los Angeles Games of 1984 consisted of 736 members. Total participants in the opening ceremonies numbered nearly 10,000. The ceremony was viewed by 92,000 spectators and an estimated 2.5 billion more on television The opening program was written by five people. This group was headed by David Wolper, producer and Tommy Walker, director. Mr. Walker also produced the ceremonies at Squaw Valley (1960) and Lake Placid (1980). Jack Elliott was the musical director and conducted his own New American Orchestra, which also participated in the opening ceremonies. Ron Field choreographed the event.

A group of 12 collegiate band directors wrote the band show. The arrangers included Tony Fox, Jack Elliott, Earl Brown, Bill Byers, Eddie Karam, and Jay Wanamaker (percussion specialist).

The marching band drill design was completed by Gordon Henderson (UCLA), Ken Dye (Rice), Walter McDaniel (Tennessee), Lee Carlson (USC), and Bartner (USC). The band consisted of 48 percussionists, 48 sousaphonists, 128 silks, and 412 wind players. Of these members two-thirds were from California colleges and universities, and the rest from other states. The students rehearsed for two weeks prior to the ceremonies for 12 hours each day.

The band was divided into two components and continued to perform at various Olympic Sites throughout the Games. The out-of-state group performed at Disneyland, Dodger Stadium, Sea World, and Magic Mountain. During the closing ceremonies the group performed traditional American marches as the athletes paraded around the stadium, as well as the Greek, United States, and Korean National Anthems.

Sarajevo, Bosnia-Herzegovina (Summer, 1984)

Among the musicians who helped open the 1984 Games in Sarajevo were three military bands which included a host of army composers/arrangers. One of the most popular themes for these Games was the *March of the Continents* comprised of a medley of favorite folk songs.

The film themes *Chariots of Fire* by Vangelis and *Gonna Fly Now* from *Rocky* conjured up images of athletes and their struggles and are included on the recording of music from the Sarajevo Games.

Calgary, Canada (Winter, 1988)

The 1988 Calgary Olympics saw the longest and most widespread arts festival to date ever held at an Olympic Games. The five week, 12.6 million dollar program, showcased the diversity of Canada's cultural heritage with more than 2,200 artists and 600 performance exhibitions. Ticket sales to the various events reached nearly $2.6 million. Contemporary and classical music were featured including performances by the Calgary Philharmonic, Edmondton Symphony, National Arts Centre Orchestra, Toronto Symphony, Esprit Orchestra, Societe de Musiqye Contemporaine du Quebec, and Calgary Youth Symphony.

Performing choirs included the Elmer Iseler Singers, Pro Coro Canada, Tudor Singers of Montréal, Vancouver Chamber Choir, The Mikaeli Chamber Choir, and Toronto Childrens Chorus. Chamber music was provided by the Julliard String Quartet, Colorado Quartet, Carlo Curley, and Corey and Katja Cerovsek. Folk music was provided by Andre-Philippe Gagnon, Michel Lemieux, the Olympic Jazz Band, and the World Drums.

Wintershow '88 was the name given to events in the Calgary area. This included performances in downtown Calgary at the noon hour.

More than 5,600 volunteers helped with the opening and closing ceremonies. Most of the more than 30 musical pieces used in these ceremonies were written and recorded in Calgary. Musicians from the area were used to make these recordings in three overdubbed components. The opening ceremony choir was comprised of 1,100 members. These performers were chosen from all over Alberta and sang *Coming Together,* the official theme of the XV Winter

Games. So inclusive was the local flavor of this event that even the Calgary Stampede Showband performed. The Royal Canadian Mounted Police performed a short version of their famous musical ride. Also heard were Ian Tyson's *Four Strong Winds* and *Alberta Bound* by Gordon Lightfoot, both Canadian recording artists. *Can't You Feel It?*, a song especially composed for the Games was also performed. Participation at these Winter Games was strong with 57 countries sending representatives.

Seoul, Korea (Summer, 1988)

A special fanfare was composed by Kim Chung-gill, professor at the National University of Seoul, for the Olympic Flag entrance into the stadium. Another professor at the National University of Seoul, Kang Suk-hee, composed *The Fire of Prometheus* which was used for the lighting (*Legend of Fire*) and extinguishing (*Harmony*) of the Olympic Flame.

Other music composed especially for the ceremonies included the following:

A World United, Chang Ik-hwan
Affection, Kim Chung-gill
Beyond the Barriers, Hwang Pyong-gi
Buds, Lee Kon-yong
Chaos, Kim Chung-gill
Dance at the Presentation of the Olympic Flag, Kim So-hee
The Dance of Hwakwan, Kim He-jo
Dance of the Lights, Choi Chang-kwon
Light of the Beginning, Choi Tong-son
Olympic Fanfare, Kim Chung-gill
Outward Bound Ships, Kim So-hee
Parade of Boats on the River Han, Kim Hee-jo
Parade of the Drum, Kang Chun-il
Prayer, Lee Saeng-gang
Prayer to the Sky and the Dance of Cha-il, Kim He-jo
The Road at Dawn, Park Pom-hun
The Sky, the Earth and the Man, Choi Tong-son
Sound and Light, Lee Ching-gu
Welcome, Kim Hee-jo

The official Olympic Song composed for the Seoul Games was Italian Giorgio Moroder's *Hand in Hand* with lyrics by American Tom Whitlock. The music of John Williams was featured once again as his *Olympic Spirit* was chosen as the NBC-TV Olympic coverage theme.

ALBERTVILLE, FRANCE (WINTER, 1992)

On October 20, Jordi Savall opened the Olympic Arts Festival with the Concert of Nations. He was known as the best gamba player in the world and was an enthusiastic organizer of the Festival of Ambronay in Ain. Savall put together a series of early music concerts that included music of Mozart, Handel, Bach, Couperin, and others of the Baroque era. Featured artists included the French soprano Montserrat Figueras.

The concert, devoted to Romantic music, featured José Van Dam (a local of the Dauphine region of France) in Berlioz' *The Damnation of Faust*. This was played by the Orchestre National de Lyon led by Emmanuel Krivine. Also featured in chamber concerts was Francophile American. The new European Strings accompanied her in Schubert's *Shepherd on the Rock*.

World premieres highlighted the Festival's Twentieth Century Music. *Asmara* and *Avoaha* were pieces commissioned by the State and composed by Jean-Louis Florentz and Maurice Ohana.

Original music by Henry Torgue and Serge Houppin was composed for the choreography of *The Legend of Romeo and Juliet* and *Don Juan* as part of the Universal Exhibition at the Cultural Olympiad.

Musical performances centered around the historical and cultural development of the region. European Music Throughout the Ages was the theme for seven concerts designed to accentuate this regional flavor. A reference work, *Noces* by Stravinsky, was performed by the Lyon Opera Orchestra and directed by Kent Nagano. On the lighter side, the musical comedy *Appelez-moi George* was presented with music composed by Catherine Lara and arranged by Eddy Rosemond.

The opening and closing ceremonies in Albertville were considered some of the most contemporary to date and included "bubble" people skating in the large outdoor arena and percussion ensemble members suspended from cranes by bungee cords. All this was performed to nearly avant garde/new age music.

The NBC team of Mike Cohen, Bill Herbstman, and Steve Haun again combined to provide music for the various athlete profiles and ceremonies. Cohen produced many of the speed skating segments including Dan Jansen's disappointing fall where Haun's *Carpe Diem* was featured.

Susan Risenger served as the music coordinator for CBS-TV Sports coverage.

Barcelona, Spain (Summer, 1992)

The official song of the 1992 Summer Games was Andrew Lloyd Webber's *Friends Forever*. The Barcelona opening ceremonies were punctuated with a performance by a group of the world's most famous opera talent, who all just happened to be Spanish! Placido Domingo, José Carreras, Montserrat Caballe, Giacomo Aragall, Teresa Berganza, and Juan Pons combined to provide a stirring and emotional medley of opera's greatest hits. This medley was referred to by some as a microcosm of the Games themselves and included:

Carmen, Bizet—*Prelude, La fleur que to m'avais jetee , Toreador, en garde!, Habanera*
La Traviata, Verdi—*Brindisi, Di Provenza*
The Tales of Hoffman, Offenbach—*Barcaolle*
La Boheme, Puccini—*Quando m'en vo*
Rigoletto, Verdi—*Bella figlia dell'amore, La donna e mobile*
Pagliacci, Leoncavalla—*Vesti la giubba*
Tosca, Puccini—*E lucevan le stelle*
Il Trovatore, Verdi—*Di quella pira*
Aida, Verdi—*Ritorna vincitor*
The Barber of Seville, Rossini—*Una voce poco fa, Largo al factotum*
Norma, Bellini—*Casta diva*

James Curnow was commissioned by the Barcelona Arts Olympiad/Committee for Organizing the Olympic Games to compose a work that was used when the Olympic Flag was brought from Barcelona to Atlanta in September of 1992.

Musical producers for the NBC-TV coverage of the Games, as well as opening and closing ceremonies, included Mike Cohen and Bill Herbstman. Steve Haun, a young, New Age composer from Boulder, Colorado wrote much of the music for the television coverage including segments for women's gymnastics, (*Renewal, Shining Through* , and *Snowdance*), women's swimming (*There is a Place for Peace*), several selections for track and field events, and athlete profiles during the closing ceremonies (*Boulder Builder Theme, Carpe Diem, Breaking Away, Dreamquest,* and *Victory*). John Colby also composed music for NBC's Barcelona coverage, and John Tesh (most noted as co-host of Entertainment Tonight) composed a selection titled *The Games*.

Lillehammer, Norway (Winter, 1994)

Following an invitation from the Nagano Committee for Organizing the Olympic Games, the Grex Vocalis Choir from Norway gave a special concert in Nagano on June 16, 1994 to help commemorate the 100th anniversary of the IOC. This choir also performed at the opening Ceremonies in Lillehammer. Well represented were original folk songs and traditional classical selections. An encore in Japanese was especially well received by the Nagano audience.

The CBS television broadcast theme music for coverage of the 1994 Winter Games in Lillehammer was composed by Tamara Kline with arrangements by Bob Christianson.

Several hundred folk dancers and 350 fiddlers were highlighted in the ski jump arena during the opening and closing ceremonies from Lillehammer. Arne Nordheim and Egil Monn-Iversen worked together as composer and musical director of the opening and closing ceremonies and provided musical consultation throughout the Olympic region. Also involved in the opening ceremonies was Sami artist Nils Aslak Valkaepaa singing a *joik* live. The *joik* is a traditional Sami chant created at a particular point in time that cannot be played back!

Traditional instruments used included the lur (a lure), the hardingfele (Hardanger fiddle), and the langeleik (the Norwegian dulcimer). The vetter, mythological beings, rose from their underground lairs to welcome participants and spectators from around the world. The entrance of the athletes was accompanied by drums of the Royal Norwegian Guard playing traditional peasant dances and the Norwegian Radio Orchestra simultaneously playing folk dances to the same rhythms.

Nils Henrik Asheim won the competition for the Olympic fanfare. The piece was written for 12 trumpets and played live at all Olympic ceremonies. The composition was based on the Hardanger fiddle tune *Bjolleslatt*, a country dance from the Valdres valley. Asheim also arranged a brass band version of the fanfare titled *Olympic Fanfare and March.*

In the closing ceremonies, Nordheim's *Magma* was performed with the *Nokken* (river sprite) symbolically rising from the watery depths. The whole ceremony, including the entrance of the athletes, became more relaxed with jazz/folk rhythms by the Bukkene Bruse folk group and the Brazz Bros ensemble.

The Olympic Arts Festival in Lillehammer centered around Maihaugen Hall, although not everything took place there. Other concert sights included Banken Cultural Centre, Cathedral Point, Hamar, the Gjovik Hall, the Olympic Park, the Hamar Theater, and several churches in the region.

An integral part of the Olympic Torch festival was the formal ceremony that took place at each spot where the torch was kept for the night. These mini festivals were the responsibility of the host community and included performances by local bands and musicians.

Ballet was an important aspect of the Olympic Arts Festival in Norway. The grand finale of the ballet programs was a performance of *Stormen* (based on the Shakespeare play by the same name) with music by Arne Nordheim and choreography by Gen Tetley. Other ballet performances included music by Edvard Grieg, Ragnar Soderlind, Synne Skouen, and Tveor Nordensten.

Norwegian life has been greatly influenced and enriched by folk music. This played an important part in both the Olympic Arts Festival and the Olympic Ceremonies. Soprano Solveig Kringlebotn created a performance titled Norsk Tonefall-for Grieg og Etter which was featured at Maihaugen Hall on Thursday, February 12. Norwegian national folk champions were featured on February 19 with champion fiddler Sondre Bratland and organist Lver Kleive playing in the region's churches on February 20. Sami Nils-Aslak Valkeapaa led a Ur-konsert at Maigaugen Hall on February 22 with indigenous artists from other lands.

Jazz music was not neglected at Lillehammer. Representatives of this idiom included pianist Bengt Hallberg (playing with the Lillehammer Mixed Choir and Haugesund choir VissJazz), the Ostre Titen Big Band (performing Helge Hurum's arrangement of *Peer Gynt Suite* by Grieg), as well as the Gli Scapoli Choir, the Jazz Guerrillas Band and the Vyrde, Klang, and area male voice choirs. Jon Balke's music was also featured for the production of *Salto: Millennium*. Not to be overlooked was the Brazz Bros jazz ensemble with Lester Bowie performing Scandinavian and Afro-American music at the Lillehammer Church on February 24.

Chamber music was also highlighted during the Lillehammer arts festival. The Greig Trio, with viola player Lars Anders Tomter, performed Brahms, Mozart, and Lase Thoresen. Cikada (a chamber ensemble with varied instrumentation) performed contemporary music of the twentieth century including works by Webern, Asheim, and Schoberg. Another chamber ensemble featuring Tomter, Russian, Alexander Rudin, and Havard Gimse performed music of C.P.E. Bach, Geirr Tveitt, Vitold Lutoslavski, Beethoven, and Brahms. Études and songs of Mozart, Ravél, and Rachmaninov were performed by Leif Ove Andsnes, Christian Tetzlaff, and Dmitri Kharitonov on February 14. The Norwegian Chamber Orchestra gave the first performance of Haflidi Hallgrimsson's work commissioned by the Lillehammer Committee for Organizing the Olympic Games (between music of Stravinsky and Mozart). Soprano Ragnhild Heiland Sorensen was the soloist and the conductor was Terje Tonnesen. Also featured during the festival was music by Miaskovski and Randall Meyers. Gerd Rindal conducted the Vingrom Choir on Sunday, February 23 and Gli Scapoli, an all-male choir on

February 28. Guests Berit Opheim and Sondre Bratland performed in the Lillehammer Church with the Oslo Chamber Choir on the February 12. A group called Geilogospel combined gospel and folk music in a concert presented on February 15. The Silver Boys choir with Anne Gjevang was featured in Ringsaker Church. Kvandal and Grieg were featured composers in the Bergen Cathedral Choir Concert with soloist Harald Bjorkoy on February 19. Thomas Caplin conducted a concert in Maihaugen Hall by the Collegeium Vocale Chamber Choir with soloists Henning Sommerro, Sven Nyhus, Aage Kvalbein, and Sigmund Groven.

Brass bands took center stage in many of the Lillehammer venues. Pianist Håkon Austbo accompanied the Brottum Musical Society with selections that included Grieg's *A Minor Concerto*. The Lillehammer Musikforening, the oldest brass band in Norway chartered nearly 130 years ago, performed in the Maihaugen Hall on January 22. The Band of the Royal Norwegian Guard was also featured in Ringebu Hall during the Olympic Arts Festival. Other brass band performances included the Lillehammer Youth Band, the Military Band of the Norwegian Defense Forces, the Oppland Janisjar Brass Band, and Aikanger-Bjorsvik Musikklag. The 1992 Krisin Cup winners gave a concert on Tuesday, February 22 at the Lillehammer Cinema. The Eikanger-Bjorsvik band with actor Jon Eikemo and folk singer Ivar Medaas performed a grand gala evening concert on Sunday, February 27 in Maigaugen Hall.

It is interesting to note that Norway has more bands per capita than any other country in the world with nearly 2,000 brass bands belonging to a federation with 120,000 musicians. The level of participation is remarkable considering it comes from a country with a population of only four million. This may have been the reason that there were more bands participating in Lillehammer than at any other Games. Since WWII the standard for wind musicians has risen steadily, providing quality musicians for both brass bands and symphony orchestras. Some claim this is due to the improvements in music education in the municipal schools, conservatories, and the Norwegian State Academy of Music, as well as the presence of a strong Norwegian Band Federation.

This strong band tradition might be traced back to early bukkehorns and prillarhorns played by goatherders, and lokker (cattle calls) sounding from mountain top to mountain top as a means to rally people or call the animals home. The first official Norwegian band was formed just outside Oslo in 1801. Many of the early bands were formed as part of a club or group of friends getting together to have a good time. The first school band was formed by William Farre who paraded his 24 musicians at the head of the school procession during the 1902 Constitution Day ceremonies. During the next six years 19 more schools bands were formed in the Oslo area alone.

The Norwegian Federation of Boys Bands was founded in 1918 and organized a performance for King Haakon VII that included 800 musicians. Today the federation exists under the name the Norwegian Band Federation (NMF) and has offices in Bergen. The staff includes 11 full-time employees, 1,300 adult, and 700 school groups.

Norwegian bands play an important part in community life. One small island town north of Bergen (Radoy) with a population of only 4,200, has six bands (three school and three adult)! Among these six groups are four National Champions and one European Champion. The NMF produced a concert during June of 1994 before the Olympics that included a grand concert by 25,000 musicians representing 530 different bands.

The most well-known modern Norwegian wind musician is Ole Edvard Antosen. His father, Odd R. Antonsen, was a band leader in Hamar north of Oslo. Ole Edvard is most noted for his 1992 CD titled *Tour de Force* which included the Mick Jager/Keith Richards song *Honky Tonk Woman*.

Other nontraditional concert opportunities during the Lillehammer Games included Dissimilis (disabled artists group), popular singers Karoline Kruger, Sigvart Dagsland, and Moren Harket, the Gjovik Sinfonietta (directed by Rolf Baekkelund), the Scandinavian Olympic Youth Orchestra, the Gvovik Town Orchestra, and Norwegian soprano Anne-Lise Bernsten with Nils Henrik Asheim.

Major orchestral concerts were presented throughout the designated Olympic region. The English Chamber Orchestra, with soloist Sigurd Slarrebrekk and conductor Ole Kristian Ruud, performed on January 15 in Oslo Concert Hall. The concert schedule during the arts festival included performances by The St. Petersburg Philharmonic (with pianist Leif Ove Andsnes and conductor Semyon Bychkov), the Stavanger Symphony Orchestra and Grant Llwellyn (with trumpeters Maurice Andre and Ole Edvard Antonsen) and the Master Meeting concert (with Coburn, Rund, and the Trondheim Symphony Orchestra playing music of Geirr Tveitt and Richard Strauss). Other programs included soprano Bodil Arnesen, pianist Roger Vignoles (performing the works of Grieg, Richard Strauss, Alnaes, Schumann, De Falla, Granados, and Donizetti), the Bergen Philharmonic with cellist Truls Mork (performing a new work by Ketil Hvoslef) and the Oslo Philharmonic conducted by Sinopoli (with works by Mahler and Strauss).

7

The Centennial

Atlanta, Georgia, USA (Summer, 1996)

Shortly after securing the Summer Games for 1996, the Atlanta Committee for Organizing the Olympic Games (ACOG) and NBC Sports (which had won the contract for televising the event) looked to a well-known and trusted composer for preparing a piece that would be truly Olympic in nature. John Williams, Oscar-winning composer and Conductor Lauriette of the Boston Pops Orchestra was commissioned by both to write his third Olympic piece. His two earlier selections, *Olympic Fanfare and Theme* (1984—Los Angeles) and *Olympic Spirit* (1988—Seoul), were tremendous successes and quickly became identified with this major sporting event. The new piece, titled *Summon the Heroes,* premiered in Boston during a series of 1995 holiday concerts by the Boston Pops with the composer conducting. In addition to other Olympic pieces, numerous symphonic works, and 75 film scores, he has composed fanfares for the 1987 International Summer Special Olympics (*We're Lookin' Good*) and for the 1989 World Alpine Ski Championships held in Vail, Colorado (*Winter Games Fanfare*).

John Williams and SONY Digital Masterworks combined with the Boston Pops Orchestra to produce the first of what could be many Olympic Centennial music recordings. The CD, taking its name from the new Olympic Theme *Summon the Heroes*, was released in mid-April, 1996. This recording was completed during a January, 1995 blizzard in Boston and includes actual Olympic pieces and music of an "Olympic" nature. Works appearing on the *Summon the Heroes* CD that have a definite link to the Olympics are, all three of Williams' Olympic themes, the Shostakovich *Festive Overture* (official theme for the 1980 Games in Moscow), Vangelis' *Chariots of Fire* (performed at the 1984 Games in Sarejevo), Josef Suk's *Toward a New Life* (recipient of the Silver Medal in the 1932 Los Angeles Games), Arnaud's *Bugler's Dream* (1968 ABC-TV Olympic coverage theme), Mikis Theodorakis' *Ode to Zeus* (commissioned by the 1992 Barcelona Olympic Committee), and Torke's *Javelin* (commissioned by the 1996 Atlanta Olympic Committee). Pieces that conjure up images of Olympicism include Carl Orff's *Carmina Burana* and Miklos Rozsa's *Parade of the Charioteers* (from the movie Ben Hur). Bernstein's *Olympic Hymn,* also on this recording, is very special in that it was commissioned by the German Olympic Committee in 1981 for the International Olympic

Congress held in Baden-Baden. It was previously recorded only informally at its inaugural performance.

As in Albertville (1992) and Lillehammer (1994), The NBC team of Cohen and Herbstman will once again produce the television coverage of the Centennial Games in Atlanta. So, in addition to the John Williams theme, more music by Steve Haun and others will complement the various athlete profiles and ceremonies. Haun will also complete an album in July, 1996 titled *Citrus, Atius, Fortius* (*Swifter, Higher, Stronger*), that will include many of the Olympic pieces used by NBC during the Games.

The Atlanta Olympic Arts Festival (AOAF), sponsored by the ACOG, was designed to be one of the largest and best festivals in recent years. The promotional brochure for the AOAF announces that "The world's greatest athletes are coming to Atlanta in the summer of 1996... and so are the world's finest performers, artists, playwrights, and composers." The AOAF is scheduled to run from June 1 through August 3, 1996. The musical highlights of the arts festival program in Atlanta include a mixture of styles and performers.

In the popular music vein James Brown, the Godfather of Soul, will be one of the featured artist at the 21 nightly Olympic Amphitheater concerts. Also included will be Trisha Yearwood, Willie Nelson, Riders in the Sky, and the western swing band Asleep at the Wheel. Gospel performers will include Sounds of Blackness and the bluegrass superstar Alison Krauss with her group Union Station. International stars will include Angelique Kidjo, Shoukicki Kina, and Wei Wei.

Classical music will be well represented through performances by the Atlanta Symphony Orchestra with Jessye Norman and the Atlanta Opera (performing Gershwin's *Of Thee I Sing)* and Itzhak Perlman. Charles Wadsworth will organize a special chamber music program.

Other musical groups and headliners include Lynryd Skynyrd, The Giants of Jazz, Travis Tritt, Yoel Levi, and William Fred Scott. Also featured will be the Australian Youth Orchestra and Atlanta Youth Orchestra in a joint program as well as a performance of Mahler's *Symphony No. 2, The Resurrection*, directed by Yoel Levi with the Atlanta Symphony and Chorus.

Soon after the announcement that Atlanta would be the site for the Centennial Games, the ACOG formed both the structure for the Cultural Olympiad and the 1996 Atlanta Olympic Band (AOB). Jeffrey N. Babcock, Ph.D. was chosen as the Cultural Olympiad Director and Bucky Johnson of Georgia Tech was named AOB director. Andrea Strauss was named Associate Director of the band and Steve Hankla, Tim Hinton, Melvin Hodges, Chris Moore, and Don Roberts were selected as Assistant Directors.

The AOB will be comprised of nearly 600 college and high school students from throughout Georgia and was initially formed in 1992. There were 70 music educators involved in this endeavor and nearly 700 people volunteered to help.

Pre-Olympic performances by the 1996 AOB include:

Olympic Flag Arrival in Savannah
Olympic Flag Jam '92 at the Georgia Dome
Olympic Flag Arrival Ceremony in Atlanta at the Underground Atlanta
Egleston Children's Christmas parades 1992, 1993, 1994
Martin Luther King parades 1993, 1994
Georgia Music Education Association/
    Southern Division Music Educators National Conference in Savannah
Clinton Inaugural Parade in Washington, D.C.
Macon Cherry Blossom Festival 1993
Georgia Olympic Day at Emory University
Georgia State games opening ceremonies—
    Mexico! A Tapestry in Piedmont Park 1993, 1994
Atlanta Falcons professional football halftime show
Bands of America regional competition at the Georgia Dome
Dedication of the Olympic Experience at the Underground Atlanta
NFL VIP Reception for Super Bowl XXVIII
St. Patrick's Day parade in Savannah 1994
Celebrate Africa-Black Arts Festival in Piedmont Park
Macy's Thanksgiving Day parade in New York City 1994

Special music composed and arranged for the AOB includes the following:

Olympic Flag Fanfare and Theme, James Curnow
Under One Flag, Jay Bocook
Atlanta '96 Olympic Salute, Mark Aramian
Blues for Izzy, Bill Locklear
Anthem for Victory, Quincy Hilliard
Olympic Gold, arranged by Tom Wallace
Pinnacle, Bill Locklear
Five Fanfares, Ron Mendola
Inno Olympico, arranged by Bill Locklear
The Olympian, Tom Wallace
Eternal Quest, Jay Dawson

The group took a short break during the fall of 1995 and spring of 1996 in anticipation of the grueling schedule required to prepare for the actual Games in the summer of 1996.

8

The Future

NAGANO, JAPAN (WINTER, 1998)

Although the Winter Games of 1998 seem to be in the distant future, Norwegian Jan Van der Roost was commissioned by the Nagano Community Band to write a piece in 1992 to commemorate its jubilee and provide a vision for the next Winter Games. The selection, *Olympica*, is dedicated to director Ikuo Inagaki and will, without a doubt, become a familiar theme for the Japanese as they prepare for the Winter Games in 1998.

Locations announced for the future Summer Olympic Games are Sidney, Australia (2000) and Salt Lake City, Utah, USA (2002).

9

Music in Olympic Skating and Gymnastics Competition

Outside of the opening ceremonies, closing ceremonies, and medal presentations, the most prominent position music assumes, at least in the general public's eye (or ear), is the background to skating and ice dancing events and during the women's gymnastics floor exercises. These have become some of the most popular competitions with television audiences throughout the world.

Figure Skating and Ice Dancing

Figure skating is the oldest sport in the Winter Olympics, having actually been included in the Summer Games beginning in 1908. It became a regular winter sport with the introduction of the Winter Games in 1924. At the 1976 Winter Games in Innsbruck, Austria, ice dancing was included for the first time.

In Carlo Fassi's book, Figure Skating, he points out the importance of music selection in the competition. Because the short program is only two minutes long, he prefers that the music be a somewhat fast tempo which allows the skater greater opportunity to execute the seven required elements in a smooth order. He also believes that coaches and skaters in recent years have become more willing to use ethnic and perhaps unusual music to enhance the short program.

Fassi likes to encourage skaters to choose their musical selections and choreography early so that they can execute the program with a high degree of expressive feeling. The five minute long program has no required elements and the skater is judged on technical and expressive merit. Each judge is looking for accuracy, firmness of balance, fluidity, composition, interpretation of the music, and the cohesiveness of the musical style and skating program. Synchronization of music and skating is a definite consideration for the judges. In many cases the music begins fast, shifts into a slower and more expressive section, and ends fast. We have seen many variations on this order however, Fassi recommends that only the most artistic skater should attempt a slow ending. Katarina Witt, at the '94 Olympic Games in Lillehammer, demonstrated one of the best "expressive" programs in recent years with her rendition of *Where Have all the Flowers Gone?*

The expressive aspect of a skater's performance cannot be overlooked. In 1994, the winner of the women's individual title was decided by the scores in the artist merit category. Nancy Kerrigan and Oksana Baiul had tied after the long program and the rules state that ties will be broken based on the higher artistic merit score.

Fassi also recommends that the transition from one musical selection to another (if using more than one piece) be smooth and nearly seamless. He dislikes varying the genre of music during the presentation. A rap-classical-jazz mix might not permit the best continuity for the skater.

Fassi suggests that the music be spliced by a highly skilled technician and that a brief musical introduction is far more effective than starting cold. In the 1994 Winter Games in Lillehammer, the English ice dancing pair of Torvill and Dean demonstrated some of these important considerations. The music used for their program was orchestrated by Dean; he even conducted the recording session to insure that the tempi were exactly what the pair wanted.

Recent skaters and the music used for their long and short programs display a variety of musical styles. As suggested by Fassi, you can see in the following list, the personalities of the skaters are usually reflected in the music they have chosen.

The following list shows some of the music the top figure skating competitors have chosen in recent Olympic Games.

Olympiad	Year	Competitor	Short/Long (Free) Program Music
XVII	1994	Oksana Baiul	Swan Lake, Tchaikovsky/Medley of Broadway show tunes
		Brian Boitano	Selections from the musical Carousel/A Lincoln Portrait and Appalachian Spring, Copeland
		Kurt Browning	/Music from the movie Casablanca
		Philippe Candeloro	/Music from the movie The Godfather
		Josee Chouinard	An American in Paris, Gershwin
		Scott Davis	Music from Zorba the Greek/Selections from the musical West Side Story, Bernstein
		Tonya Harding	Music from the movie Much Ado About Nothing/Music from the movie Jurassic Park
		Nancy Kerrigan	Desperate Love, composed for her by Mark Militano/Medley of Neil Diamond tunes
		Chen Lu	Claire de Lune, Debussy/Music from the movie The Mission
		Aren Nielson	/Music from the movie The Rocketeer
		Victor Petrenko	Toreador Song from the opera Carmen/La donna é mobile from the opera Rigoletto; Ah fors e lui from the opera La Traviata
		Elvis Stojko	Frogs in Space/Music from the movie Dragon
		Alexei Urmanov	Selections from the opera Rigoletto/Selections from the opera The Barber of Seville
		Katarina Witt	Music from the movie Robin Hood: Prince of Thieves/Where Have all the Flowers Gone?
		Brasseur and Eisler	Hungarian Dance No. 5, Brahms/Rhapsody on a Theme of Paganini, Rachmaninoff
		Mishkutenok and Dmitriev	Don Quixote, Minkus/Piano Concerto No. 2, Rachmaninoff
		Gordeeva and Grinko	Medley of flamenco tunes/Pathetique Piano Sonata and Moonlight Piano Sonata, Beethoven
		Shishkova and Naumov	Overture and waltz from Die Fliedermaus, Strauss/Warsaw Concerto, Addinsell
		Kovarikov and Novotny	Overture to La Forza del Destino, Verdi
		Torvill and Dean	History of Love/Let's Face the Music and Dance
		Usova and Zhulin	Selections from La Strada
		Rahkano and Kokko	Rhumba, Edmundo Ross/Selections from La Strada
		Wotzel and Steuer	/Rock Around the Clock and Hummingbird
		Navka and Gezolian	/Medley from the movie Strictly Ballroom
XVI	1992	Kristi Yamaguchi	/Malaguena
XV	1988	Katarina Witt	/Selections from the opera Carmen
		Debbie Thomas	/Selections from the opera Carmen
XIV	1984	Torvill and Dean	Capriccio Espagnol/Bolero, Ravél
XIII	1980	Torvill and Dean	/In the Mood

Gymnastics

Women's gymnastics became a recognized Olympic sport in 1952. The women's floor exercise is the only gymnastic event to use a musical background. One of the most well-known original pieces used in Olympic competition is *Nadia's Theme*, composed especially for Nadia Comaneci in 1976 when she won the bronze medal.

Denise Gula, in her book Dance Choreography for Competitive Gymnastics, lists several steps for the gymnast to follow in choosing the floor routine music.

- Musical style should fit the physical stature and personality of the gymnast. For instance, a small, petite competitor should not choose grand, majestic music.
- The competitor should stay away from well-known movie themes and would be better off to choose music that is somewhat obscure—one big vote here for originality!
- Music that is too trite lacks the opportunity to be creative and restricts movement.
- Musical phrases are of the utmost importance. Bad musical phrasing creates difficulty in timing. The gymnast is encouraged to choose music that has logical sections that will complement the tumbling exercises.

The floor exercise requirements state that there must be both slow and fast movements, within the required time frame of only 70–90 seconds. The judges will be looking for music that complements everything that the gymnast will be doing during the exercise.

After choosing the music, the gymnast must determine which movement style (jazz, ballet, folk, or character) best fits. It is possible that a popular musical selection would permit many different styles of expression. Gula also suggests that the routine have a theme dependent on the music style and tempo chosen and an introduction, main body, and closing. The musical selection must provide a good structure, underlying and reinforcing the shape of the exercise.

Postlude

Without a doubt music will continue to provide an important function at the modern Olympic Games. Even if the old Olympic Arts Competitions are not reinstated, music will play an important part in the Olympic Ceremonies and as an inspiration for athletes in all events. We cannot neglect the special aesthetic touch music adds to events such as ice skating and gymnastics. As the Games draw the world closer together, we will see an ever increasing interest in the cultural diversity represented in the arts festivals and in de Coubertin's philosophy that these Games should embody the "mind and the spirit."

Music List

Summer Games

Olympiad	Year	City	Music	Composer/Arranger	Purpose/Comments
I	1896	Athens	Loghengrin	Wagner	Opening Ceremony
			The Olympic Hymn	Spiro Samaras, Kostis Palamos	Official Hymn
			Pentathalon	Dionysios Lavrangas	Incidental
			The Sailor Lad		
II	1900	Paris	No Specific Citations		
III	1904	St. Louis	Along the Plaza	Henry K. Hadley	
			Hymn of the West	John Knowles Paine	Official World's Fair Hymn
			Louisiana March	Frank Van der Stucken	
			Music made popular by professional traveling concert band's of the time, such as John Philip Sousa		
IV	1908	London	Dorando	Irving Berlin	
V	1912	Stockholm	Triumphant Olympic March**	H. Alexandersson	Opening and Closing
			Triumphal Olympic March	Ricardo Barthelemy	Gold Medal winner
			Valse Boston for the Olympiska Spelen	Theodor Pinet	
			Carmen, Romeo and Juliet, Tosca, lohengrin, The Tales of Hoffman, La Boheme		Royal Opera performances
VI	1916	Berlin	Canceled		
VII	1920	Antwerp	Epinicion	Oreste Riva	Silver Medal winner
			Olympic Hymn	Pierre Benoit	Official Hymn
			Olympique	G. Monier	Gold Medal winner
VIII	1924	Paris	Chasse a courre	L. Ruby Reynolds-Lewis	Music competition entry
			Deux Choeurs	Tourcoing	
			Hymne aux Sports	Gerry	Music competition entry
			Jeux Funeraires	S. Daneau	Music competition entry
			Les Jeux Olympiques	Jules Hubert	Unclear if this was performed during the ceremonies
			Ludus pro Patria	Masquillier Thiriez	Music competition entry
			Marche Sportive pour piano	J. Richard	Music competition entry
			Now Let the Games Begin	G. Bamber	Music competition entry
			Ski-Sporten	M. Moaritz	Music competition entry
IX	1928	Amsterdam	Chant du Drapeau	Gerrit Van Weezel	Perfomed by 1,200 people, Official Hymn
			Symphong No. 2, Hellas	Rudolf Simonsen	Bronze Medal winner
			Op ter Olympiade	Joh. P. Koppen	Ceremonies
X	1932	Los Angeles	Olympic Hymn	Bradley Keeler	Official Hymn
			Olympiad Welcome	Maurice Eisner and Jessica Lewis	Ceremonies
			Toward a New Life*	Josef Suk	Silver Medal winner
XI	1936	Berlin	Adagio from Hymn to Apollo	Haydn	
			Andante cantabile from the A Major Symphony	Beethoven	Ceremonies

* See Appendix A—Recordings of Olympic Music
** See Appendix B—Musical Scores

Summer Games

Olympiad	Year	City	Music	Composer/Arranger	Purpose/Comments
XI	1936	Berlin	Assai agitato	Robert Schumann	IOC Meeting
			Bergsuite	Jaroslav Krika	Bronze Medal winner
			A Dance Suite	Handel	
			Chaconne from Paris and Helen	Gluck	
			Der Laufer	Harald Genzmer	Bronze Medal winner
			Einzug der Olympia-Kampfer	Herbert Blume	Ceremonies March Music
			Herakles**	Handel	
			Il vincitore	Lino Liviabella	Silver Medal winner
			Kantate zur Olympiade 1936	Kurt Thomas	Silver Medal winner
			National Anthems**		Official anthems for the Games
			Olympic Hymn	Richard Strauss	Official Hymn, Ceremonies
			Olympische Festmusik	Werner Egk	Gold Medal winner
			Olympischer Schwur	Paul Hoffer	Gold Medal winner
			Pavanne	Schein	
					The official Olympic Film of the 1936 Games has original music composed by Walter Gronostay and Herbert Windt
XII	1940	Japan	Canceled		
XIII	1944	London	Canceled		
XIV	1948	London	Barenjagd for Orchestra	Kalervo Tuukanen	Silver Medal winner
			Canata-Friedenslaufer	Jan Zdenek Bartos	Music competition entry
			Divertimento for Flute and Streicher	Jean Weinzweig	Silver Medal winner
			Hallelujah Chorus from The Messiah	Handel	Opening Ceremony
			Kraft for Orchestra	Erling Brene	Bronze Medal winner
			Londonderry Air	Traditional with words by Sir Alan Herbert	
			Non Nobis Domine	Roger Quilter, Rudyard Kipling	Official Hymn
			Olympic Hymn	Gabriele Bianchi	Bronze Medal winner
			Olympijska Symphony	Zbrigniew Turski	Gold Medal winner
			Toccata for Klavier	Sergio Lauricella	Bronze Medal winner
XV	1952	Helsinki	A Finnish Prayer	Tanelo Kuusisto	
			Olympic Fanfare**	Aarre Merikanto	
			Olympic Hymn	Jaakko Linjama	Offical Hymn, Opening and Closing Ceremonies
			Song of the Athenians	Jean Sibelius	Closing Ceremony
XVI	1956	Melbourne	Music by several other classical composers (Tschaikovsky Concerto No.1, Schumann Concerto)	Bach, Holst, Elgar, Beethoven, Borodin, Verdi, Rossini, and Austrailians Clive Douglas, Margaret Sutherland, and Dorian Le Gallienne	
			The Messiah	Handel	Arts Festivals

* See Appendix A—Recordings of Olympic Music
** See Appendix B—Musical Scores

Summer Games

Olympiad	Year	City	Music	Composer/Arranger	Purpose/Comments
XVI	1956	Melbourne	Olympic Hymn**	Michal Spisak	Official Hymn, Ceremonies
XVI	1956	Cortina D'Ampezzo	Olympic Hymn	Michal Spisak	Official Hymn
			Olympic Parade	Giuseppe Blanc	
XVII	1960	Rome	March of the Olympians**	Tommy Walker and Robert Linn	Ceremonies
			Olympic Fanfare (taken from *Hymn of the Sun*, at the opening of Maascagni's opera *Iris*)	Maascagni	
			Olympic Hymn**	Spiro Samaras, Kostis Palamas	Official Hymn used at the first Games in 1896
XVIII	1964	Tokyo	Auld Lang Syne	traditional	Closing Ceremony
			Bravura	C.E. Duble	Opening Ceremony
			Celebration March	I. Dan	Opening Ceremony
			El Capítan	John Philip Sousa	Opening Ceremony
			Fanfare des Jeux Olympics**	Mitsuya Imai	
			Hands Across the Sea	John Philip Sousa	Opening Ceremony
			March Olympique**	Yuji Koseki	
			March Regiment	Morney	Opening Ceremony
			Old Comrades	Karl Teike	Opening Ceremony
			Olympic March	Koseki	Opening Ceremony
			Olympic Music	Osamu Shimizu and Ron Ogura	
			Olympic Overture**	Ikuma Dan	
			On the Quarter Deck	K.J. Alford	Opening Ceremony
			Our Director	F.E. Bigelow	Opening Ceremony
			Sabre and Spear	H. Starke	Opening Ceremony
			Sambre et Meuse	Planquette	Opening Ceremony
			The Tokyo Olympic Hymn**	Osamu Shimizu, Ron Ogura	Official Theme
			Zeppelin	Karl Teike	Opening Ceremony
XIX	1968	Mexico	Bugler's Dream	Leo Arnaud	Used for several years as the ABC TV Olympic Theme, Official Theme
			Guadalajara	traditional	
			La Negra	traditional	
			La Zandunga	traditional	Opening Ceremony
			Las Golondrinas	traditional	
			Sakura		Opening Ceremony
			Symphony No. 9, Finale	Beethoven	Closing Ceremony
XX	1972	Munich	Ekecheirija	Kyrsztof Penderecke	
			Gruss der Jugend	Karl Orff	Opening Ceremony
			Hymn to Sport**	Nic Niobe	
			Incidental music	Peter Herbolzheimer, Dieter Reith, and Jerry van Rooyen	

* See Appendix A—Recordings of Olympic Music
**See Appendix B—Musical Scores

Summer Games

Olympiad	Year	City	Music	Composer/Arranger	Purpose/Comments
XX	1972	Munich	Olympic Fanfare	Herbert Rehbein	
			Olympic Flame Music	Wilhelm Killmayer	
			Olympic Music	Alfred Goodman	Official Theme
			Parade of Nations	Kurt Edelhagen	Opening Ceremony
XXI	1976	Montréal	Aupres de ma blonde		
			Bayrischer Defilir		
			Cantata	Louis Chantigny	
			Chimes*		
			Closing Ceremonies Excerpts*		Closing Ceremony
			Concerto No. 3	Andre Mathieu	
			Dance of the Gymnasts*		
			Dance of the Olympic Rings*		
			Danse de la plongeuse	Andre Mathieu	
			Danse des ceintures		
			Danse Sauvage	Andre Mathieu	Closing Ceremony
			Indian Suite*		
			March of the Athletes*	Andre Mathieu	Opening Ceremony, Olympic Hymn
			Marianne s'en va-t-au moulin		
			Mistassini	Andre Mathieu	
			Olympic Hymn	Spiros Samaras, Kostis Palamas	Official Hymn
			Opening Ceremonies Excerpts*		Opening Ceremony
			Reel des cinq jumelles		
			Stern Polka		
			Trumpet feature		Performed by trumpeter Maynard Ferguson
			White Rock*	Rock Wakeman	Music for the documentary film about the 1976 Games
XXII	1980	Moscow	Festive Overture	Dimitri Shostakovich	Opening Ceremony, Olympic Theme
			Goodby Moscow	Alexandra Pakhutova	Closing Ceremony
			Ode to Sport**	Eduard Artemyev	
XXIII	1984	Los Angeles	A Chance for Heaven*	Christopher Cross	Ceremonies
			A Chorus Line	Edward Kleban	Opening Ceremony
			America (from *West Side Story*)	Bernstein	Opening Ceremony
			American the Beautiful	Ward	Opening Ceremony
			Basin Street Blues	traditional	Opening Ceremony
			Beat It	Michael Jackson	Opening Ceremony
			Bugler's Dream*	Leo Arnaud	Ceremonies
			Cheek to Cheek	Berlin	Opening Ceremony
			Conquest	Alfred Newman	Oath Music
			Courtship*	Bob James	Ceremonies

* See Appendix A—Recordings of Olympic Music
** See Appendix B—Musical Scores

Summer Games

Olympiad	Year	City	Music	Composer/Arranger	Purpose/Comments
XXIII	1984	Los Angeles	Fame	Pitchford	Opening Ceremony
			Fanfare for the Common Man	Copland	Opening Ceremony
			Fanfare Olympique	John Williams	All Ceremonies, Official Theme
			Grace*	Quincy Jones	Ceremonies
			Hoedown	Copeland	Opening Ceremony
			How the West Was Won	Alfred Newman	Opening Ceremony
			I Got Rhythm	Gershwin	Opening Ceremony
			I'm Gettin' Sentimental Over You	George Bassman	Opening Ceremony
			In the Mood	Joe Garland	Opening Ceremony
			It Don't Mean a Thing If It Ain't Got That Swing	Ellington and Mills	Opening Ceremony
			Junku*	Herbie Hancock	Ceremonies
			Let's Face the Music	Berlin	Opening Ceremony
			Manhattan	Rogers and Hart	Opening Ceremony
			Moodio*	Toto	Ceremonies
			Moonlight Serenade	Glenn Miller	Opening Ceremony
			Nothing's Gonna Stop You Now*	Loverboy	Ceremonies
			Olympian	Philip Glass	Torch Lighting Ceremony
			The Olympian**	David Chesky	Electronic Music Suite
			One	Hamlisch	Opening Ceremony
			One O'Clock Jump	Count Basie	Opening Ceremony
			Opus 1	Sy Oliver	Opening Ceremony
			Power*	Bill Conti	Ceremonies
			Reach Out and Touch (Somebody's Hand)	Diana Ross	Opening Ceremony
			Reach Out*	Giorgio Moroder	Ceremonies
			Rhapsody in Blue	Gershwin	Opening Ceremony
			Singin' in the Rain	Brown and Freed	Opening Ceremony
			Street Thunder*	Foreigner	Ceremonies
			Strike Up the Band	Gershwin	Opening Ceremony
			Waitin' On the Robert E. Lee	Lewis Muir	Opening Ceremony
			Way Down Yonder in New Orleans	Turner Layton	Opening Ceremony
			Welcome	Marvin Hamlisch	Opening Ceremony
			When the Saints Go Marchin' In	traditional	Opening Ceremony
XXIV	1988	Seoul	Fight	The Bunburys	Ceremonies
			Hand in Hand	Moroder and Whitlock	Official Olympic Song and Theme
			Harvest for the World	The Christians	Ceremonies
			Indestructible	The Four Tops	Ceremonies
			Olympic Joy	Kashif	Ceremonies
			Olympic Spirit	John Williams	Ceremonies, NBC-TV Theme

* See Appendix A—Recordings of Olympic Music
** See Appendix B—Musical Scores

Summer Games

Olympiad	Year	City	Music	Composer/Arranger	Purpose/Comments
XXIV	1988	Seoul	One Moment in Time*	Whitney Houston	Ceremonies
			Peace in Our Time	Jennifer Holliday	Ceremonies
			Reason to Try	Eric Carmen	Ceremonies
			Rise to the Occasion	Jermaine Jackson	Ceremonies
			Shape of Things to Come	Bee Gees	Ceremonies
			That's What Dreams are Made Of	Odds and Ends	Ceremonies
			Willpower	Taylor Dayne	Ceremonies
XXV	1992	Barcelona	Amigos Para Siempre	Andrew Lloyd Webber	Special Theme for the Games, Official Theme
			Barcelona Games Medley*		
			The Games	John Tesh	Used by NBC TV for coverage of the Games
			Olympic Flag Transfer	James Curnow	Transfer of Olympic Flag to Atlanta
XXVI	1996	Atlanta	A Mirror of the Day and of the Night	Antonio Zepeda	Mexico: A Cultural Tapestry
			Anahuac	Juan Ramirez	Mexico: A Cultural Tapestry
			Anthem for Victory	Quincy Hilliard	
			Atlanta 1996 Olympic Salute	Mark Aramian	All premiered by AOB
			Bird of the Heart	Lasse Thorensen	Olympic Winterland by Grieg Trio
			Blues for Izzy	Bill Locklear	Olympic Band
			Concerto No. 1	Edvard Bull	
			Der Rosebkavalier	Richard Strauss	
			Eternal Quest	Jay Dawson	
			The Explorer	Jim Oliverio	Olympic Winterland by Atlanta Symphony Orchestra
			Five Fanfares	Ron Mendola	
			Four Songs	Edvard Grieg	Olympic Winterland by Atlanta Symphony Orchestra
			The Genius of Ellington	David Baker and Gunther Schuller, directors	Smithsonian Jazz Orchestra
			In Honor of 3000	Weisenberg	Jerusalem Symphony Orchestra
			Inno Olimpico	Arranged by Bill Locklear	
			Introduction and Allegro	Elgar	
			Journey to Atlanta	Eddie Horst	Atlanta Youth Orchestra
			Music for Cello and Orchestra	Maazel	
			The Olympian	Tom Wallace	
			Of Thee I Sing	George Gershwin	Arts Olympiad Atlanta Opera
			Olympic Flag Fanfare and Theme	James Curnow	Flag Arrival by Olympic Band
			Olympic Gold	Arranged by Tom Wallace	
			Piano Concerto No. 1	Dimitri Shostakovich	
			Piano Concerto No. 1	Brahms	
			Pinnacle	Bill Locklear	

* See Appendix A—Recordings of Olympic Music
** See Appendix B—Musical Scores

Summer Games

Olympiad	Year	City	Music	Composer/Arranger	Purpose/Comments
XXVI	1996	Atlanta	Sonata for Trumpet and Strings	Purcell	London Chamber Orchestra
			Summon the Heroes	John Williams	Ceremonies
			Symphonic Dances (from *West Side Story*)	Bernstein	
			Symphony No. 10	Dimitri Shostakovich	Arts Olympiad Australian Youth Orchestra
			Symphony No. 2	Brahms	Arts Olympiad—Barvarian Radio Symphony
			Symphony No. 2	Hanson	
			Symphony No. 2, The Resurrection	Mahler	Atlanta Symphony Orchestra and Chorus
			Symphony No. 4	Tchaikovsky	
			Symphony No. 5	Prokofiev	
			Symphony No. 7	Bruckner	
			Till Eulenspiegel	Richard Strauss	
			Trio in F Minor, Op. 65	Antonin Dvorak	Olympic Winterland by Grieg Trio
			Trio in G Major	Haydn	Olympic Winterland by Grieg Trio
			Trumpet Concerto in E-Flat	Haydn	
			Umoja: Each One of Us Counts	Alvin Singleton	
			Under One Flag	Jay Bocook	
			Variations on a Theme of Corelli	Tippett	
			Various selections	Bukkene Bruse and the Foxfire Boys, Jon Balke Orchestra, Sissel Kyrkjebo, Bel Canto, and the Atlanta Super Choir	Olympic Winterland
			Various selections	Montreaux Jazz, Swiss Movement, Alder Bruder	Switzerland Festival
			Various selections	Etta Baker, John Cephas, Phil Wiggins,	Mexico: A Cultural Tapestry
			Various selections	Ladysmith Black Mambazo, Youssou N'Dour, Black Umfolosi	Celebrate Africa!
			Various selections	José Gutierrez and Friends, Cafe Tacuba, Quetzacoatl	Mexico: A Cultural Tapestry

* See Appendix A—Recordings of Olympic Music
** See Appendix B—Musical Scores

Winter Games

Olympiad	Year	City	Music	Composer/Arranger	Purpose/Comments
I	1924	Chamonix	No Specific Citations		
II	1928	St. Moritz	No Specific Citations		
III	1932	Lake Placid	No Specific Citations		
IV	1936	Garmisch-Partenkirchen	Much of the same music from the XIth Summer Games was used here		
V	1948	St. Mortiz	No Citations		
VI	1952	Oslo	Non Nobis Domine	Roger Quilter, Rudyard Kipling	Official Hymn
			Olympic Fanfare**	Johannes Hanssen	Also adaptation for Signal Theme
VII	1956	Stockholm	Fanfares from Kungarop from Marcia Carolus Rex	Swedish Cavalry March	Signal the opening of the Games, Official Hymn
VIII	1960	Squaw Valley	Conquest		
			God of Our Fathers		
			No Man is an Island		Closing Ceremony
			Ode Triumphant		Closing Ceremony
			Parade of the Olympians**	Tommy Walker and Robert Linn	Ceremonies (The U.S. Marine Band was the official band of these games and may have arrangments on file of each of these pieces)
IX	1964	Innsbruck	3rd Regiment's March	Schneider	Opening Ceremony
			47th Regiment March	Wagner	Opening Ceremony
			Celebration Music	Viktor Hruby	Opening Ceremony
			Festival Music	Karl Piliss	Opening Ceremony
			Frisch	Pesch	Opening Ceremony
			O du mein Osterreich	Preiss	Opening Ceremony
			Olympiamarsch	Labsky	Opening Ceremony
			Paradedefiliermarsch	Ambrosch	Opening Ceremony
			Rechts-schaut March	Tanzer	Opening Ceremony
			Salute to Luxemburg	Pazke	Opening Ceremony
			Schonfeldmarsch	Ziehrer	Opening Ceremony
X	1968	Grenoble	Chant Olympic	Francis Lai	Sung by Mireille Mathieu
			Music by various artists	Ella Fitzgerald, Gilbert Becaud, Charles Aznavour, Manitas de Plata, Johnny Halliday	Part of the Grenoble Entertainment Festival during the Games.
XI	1972	Sapporo	Fanfare of the Sapporo Winter Games	Akira Miyoshi	
			Farewell Song	Yoshinao Nakada	
			Hymn for the Opening Ceremony	Shuntaro Tanigawa	Opening Ceremony
			The Land of Glorious Snow	Minoru Shimizu	
			Music for the Olympic Flag Transfer	Yuji Koseki	Transfer of Olymipc Flag to Innsbruck
			Music Honoring the Emperor	Osamu Shimzu	

* See Appendix A—Recordings of Olympic Music
** See Appendix B—Musical Scores

Winter Games

Olympiad	Year	City	Music	Composer/Arranger	Purpose/Comments
XI	1972	Sapporo	The Rainbow and Snow	Saburo Iwakawa	
			Sapporo Olympic March	Naozumi Yamamoto	
XII	1976	Innsbruck	Music of *Wiltener*, (Innsbruck's traditional band)		Led by Professor Sepp Tanzer
XIII	1980	Lake Placid	Hymn to the Sacred Olympic Flame		Words from Pindar's Olympian VII ode
			Jazzmobile	Frank Foster	Ceremonies
			Kinesis	William Conti	Ceremonies
			The Man in the Middle	Tom "Harley" Campbell	Folk Tunes Ceremony
			Round a Common Corner	Lucas Foss	For documentary film
			Snow Blind	Walt Michael	Folk Tunes Ceremony
			Whiteface Reel	Tom McReesh	Folk Tunes Ceremony
XIV	1984	Sarejevo	Chariots of Fire	Vangelis	
			Gonna Fly Now, Theme from Rocky		
			Ode to Joy	Beethoven	
			World Games	John Denver	
			XVI ZOI 1984 Sarajevo: Jugoslavenska muzika		
XV	1988	Calgary	Alberta Bound	Gordon Ligthfoot	
			Can't You Feel It		
			Coming Together		Official Theme Song
			Four Strong Winds	Ian Tyson	
			Olympic Spirit	John Williams	NBC-TV Theme
			Winter Games*	David Foster	
					Music available in City of Calgary Archives
XVI	1992	Albertville	Asmara	Jean-Louis Florentz and Maurice Ohana	
			Avoaha	Jean-Louis Florentz and Maurice Ohana	
			The Damnation of Faust	Berlioz	Special Concert
			Don Juan		
			The Legend of Romeo and Juliet	Henry Torgue and Serge Houppin	Cultural Olympiad
			Music by Jordi Savall, Cantlonian Composer		
			Noces	Stravinsky	
			Shepard on the Rock	Schubert	Special Concert
XVII	1994	Lillehammer	CBS TV Theme	Tamara Kline arranged by Bob Christianson	
			Joik	Nils Aslak Valkeapaa	Olympic Fanfare winner, Opening Ceremony
			Magma	Nordheim	Closing Ceremony
			OHM, Varder and Acantus Firmus	Arne Hordheim	
			Peer Gynt Suite	Edvard Grieg	Performed several times during the games
			The Meeting Place		

* See Appendix A—Recordings of Olympic Music
** See Appendix B—Musical Scores

Winter Games

Olympiad	Year	City	Music	Composer/Arranger	Purpose/Comments
XVII	1994	Lillehammer	Venit rex!	Arne Nordheim	Entry of the King at both Ceremonies
			The World of the Sami People		Closing Ceremony
			Most of the Opening and Closing Ceremony music was traditional folk music of Norway		
XVIII	1998	Nagano	Olympica	Jan Van der Roost	Commemorate the Jubilee of the Nagano Community Band

* See Appendix A—Recordings of Olympic Music
** See Appendix B—Musical Scores

APPENDIX

Appendix A

Recordings of Olympic Music

Peter Young, ***Music for Montreal***, Recording by the Ronnie Hazlehurst Orcehstra on BBC Records, England.

1988 Summer Olympics: One Moment in Time, New York, New York: Arista Records, 1988.
Includes:
Olympic Spirit, John Williams
One Moment in Time, Whitney Huston
Fight (no matter how long), The Bunburys
Indestructible, Four Tops
Reason to Try, Eric Carmen
Shape Of Things To Come, Bee Gees
Peace In Our Time, Jennifer Holliday
Willpower, Taylor Dayne
That's What Dreams Are Made Of, Odds and Ends
Harvest For The World, The Christians
Rise to the Occasion, Jermaine Jackson and LA LA
Olympic Joy, Kashif

XXVth Olympic Games 1992: Barcelona Spain, Ediciones RTEM.
Includes:
Songs and music

A l'occasion des XViEme jeux Olympique d'Hiver, Frankfurt, Germany: Musik Nic Niobe, Edition Deffu Ton Verlag, 1988 (piano and tenor soloist).

Chansons Olympiques, Grenoble, SHTX 340595, 1968.

Domingo, Carreras, Caballé—Barcelona Games, New York: RCA, 09026/61204-2.
Includes:
Olympic Medley
12 newly recorded operatic favorites

Ekecheiriji, Warsaw: Polskie Radio Studio Eksperymentalne.

Erick Kunzel and the Cincinnati Pops, ***Pomp and Pizazz***, Cleveland: Telarc, Commerce Park Road, Cleveland, Ohio 44122, CS-30122.
Includes:
Toward a New Life, Josef Suk
Olympic Fanfare (1984), John Williams

Fanfare March, Polydor 2041 203.

Frederick Fennell, The Cleveland Symphonic Winds, Cleveland: Telarc, Commerce Park Road, Cleveland, Ohio 44122, DG-10050.
Includes:
Olympic Theme, Leo Arnaud
La Chasse, Leo Arnaud
Olympiad, Leo Arnaud

Hand in Hand: 1988 Seoul Olympic Song, Seoul, Korea: Polydor, LP 836 111-1, 1988, performed by Koreana.

Himnes nacionals, ***Banda Municipal de Barcelona***, Madrid, Spain: Ediciones, RTEM, 1992. Also, Vogue, VG 403 590495.

Hymn to Sport, Frankfurt/Main, Germany: Edition Deffu Ton Verlag, 1988

Innsbruck, PR Records, PR 131724, 1964 and 1976.

Jeux de la XXI Olympiade, Montreal 1976, Montreal: RCA.
Includes:
Opening Ceremony Excerpts
Chimes
O Canada
Dance of the Gymnasts

Closing Ceremonies Excerpts
Dance of the Olympic Rings
Indian Suite
March of the Athletes (five movements)

Moscow 1980, Balkanton BXA 10553 and BTA 10556.

The Official Music of the XXI Olympiad, Montreal, RCA, Ltd., 1976, original music from the Official Ceremonies.

The Official Music of the XXIIIrd Olympiad Los Angeles 1984, Columbia Records, CBS, 51 West 52 Street, New York, New York. PCT 39322.
Includes:
Olympic Fanfare and Theme, John Williams
A Chance for Heaven, Christopher Cross
Courtship, Bob James
Moodido (the Match), Toto
Reach Out, Giorgio Moroder
Grace, Quincy Jones
Junku, Herbie Hancock
Street Thunder, Foreigner
Power, Bill Conti
The Olympian, Philip Glass
Bugler's Dream, Loverboy
Nothing's Gonna Stop You Now, Loverboy

Orchestra of Kurt Edelhagen, GEMA 2437146.

Parade of Nations, Polydor Stereo, 2371 296 LP/3150273 CS.

Tokyo 1964, Polydor 46150, LPHM.

Salute to the Olympians, BMG Direct, DPK1-0855, 1988.

XIV ZOI 1984 Sarajevo: Jugoslavenska muzika, Sarajevo, Yugoslavia: Diskoton, LP08115, 1984.

In addition this listing, recordings have been made of some of the music from the following Games:
Melbourne, 1956
Innsbruck, 1964 and 1976
Tokyo, 1964
Grenoble, 1968
Munich, 1972
Montreal, 1976
Moscow, 1980
Los Angeles, 1984
Seoul, 1988
Albertville, 1992
Lillehammer, 1994

Video Tapes

1992 Winter Olympics Highlights, Los Angeles, CA: CBS, Inc., CBS Video, Los Angeles, CA, distributed by Fox Video, 1992.

Chronicle of the High Points and Disappointments of the 15th Winter Games with Jim McKay, 1988.

Chrysler Corporation Presents the Official 1992 Winter Olympics Highlights, CBS Sports, produced by Alan Brum and David Stern, notes by Tim McCarver and Paula Zahn.

Great Moments at the Winter Games, 1988.

The Immortals, 1988.

The Official 1988 Calgary Winter Olympics, Livonia, Michigan: ABC Sports, Inc., CBS/Fox Video, 1988.

Olympic Alpine Skiing, 1979.

Olympische Spiele, Los Angeles, California: Olympia Video Recording, produced and directed by Leni Riefenstahl, Embassy Home Entertainment, 1984. Highlights of the 1936 Games in Berlin Note: English version of the motion picture.

Appendix B

Musical Scores

Artmyev, Eduard, ***Ode to Sport***, Moscow: Moscow Union of Composers, 103009.

Chesky, David, ***The Olympian***, Manhattan Production Music Recording.

Dan, Ikuma, ***Olympic Overture***, Estera Music Publishing Company, Japan Broadcasting.

Fauré, Gabriel (1845–1924), ***Hymne 'a Apollon***, Performed at the 1894 Olympic Congress in Paris, Greek words composed about 278 BC, found engraved in marble at Delphi, Greece.

Handel, ***Herakles***, various

Hanssen, Johannes, ***Olympic Fanfare***, Norwegian Broadcasting Corporation.

Imai, Mitsuya, ***Fanfare des Jeux Olympics***, Estera Music Publishing Company, Japan Broadcasting.

Koseki, Yuji, ***March Olympique***, Estera Music Publishing Company, Japan Broadcasting.

Linjama, Jaako, ***Olympic Hymn***, Findland: 1952, text by Toivo Lyy.

Merikanto, Aarre, ***Olympic Fanfare***, BBC Archives.

Michel, Spisak, ***Olympic Hymn***, Polish.

Miyoshi, Akira, ***Fanfare of the Sapporo Winter Games***, Japan: Onagaku No Tomo sha Corporation.

Niobe, Nic, ***Hymn to Sport***, Frankfurt/Main Germany: Deffu-Ton-Verlag, 1972.

Samaras, Spiros (1861–1917), ***Hymne Olympiiakos***, Lausanne, Switzerland: IOC, 1896.

Shimizu, Osamu, ***The Tokyo Olympic Hymn***, Estera Music Publishing Company, Japan Broadcasting.

Strauss, Richard (1864–1949), ***Olympische hymne (Song in C Major)***, Berlin: Forstner, 1936, text by Robert Lubahan.

Walker, Tommy, and Ling, Robert, ***March of the Olympians***, The Walt Disney Company.

Walker, Tommy, and Ling, Robert, ***Parade of the Olympians***, The Walt Disney Company.

Williams, John, ***The Olympic Spirit,*** Warner Bros., 1988

________, various national anthems, Leipzig: Verlag Breitkopf and Hartel

Bibliography

Austin, Terry, ***Bands at the 1904 World's Fair—College Band Directors National Association Journal***, New Haven, Connecticut: Number 10, Spring/Summer 1994, pp. 23–29.

Barker, Philip, ***Sport in Music—Olympic Review***, December, 1992, pp. 608–609.

de Navacelle, Geoffroy, Pierre de Coubertin, ***The Man, His Family, His Time—Olympic Review,*** Lausanne, Switzerland: Vol. 25, No. 4. p. 47, August/September, 1995.

Durry, Jean, ***Pierre De Coubertin: Sport and Aesthetics—Olympic Review***, 1986, pp. 390–396.

Fassi, Carlo, ***Figure Skating with Carlo Fassi***, New York: Scribner, 1980

Gula, Denise A., ***Dance Choreography for Competitive Gymnastics***, Champaign, IL: Leisure Press, A Division of Human Kinetics Publishers, 1990.

Hohne, Erhard, ***Music and Sport—Olympic Review***, 1979, pp. 437–439.

Killanin, Lord and Rodda, John, ***The Olympic Games***, London: Barrie and Jenkins, ISBN 214-200914, 1976.

Levitt, Susanna Halpert, ***1984 Olympic Arts Festival***, theater, 1990.

Mathys, Fritz K., ***Sport and Music—Olympic Review***, October, 1985, pp. 628–631.

Schmitt, Oliver, ***Watched by the World—Olympic Review***, January, 1992, pp. 18–20.

Wanamaker, Jay, ***The All-American Olympic Marching Band—The Instrumentalist***, January 1985, pp.37–44.

________, ***A Music Teacher's Approach to the Olympics—Music Educators Journal***, hints on an interdisciplinary approach to music.

________, ***Die Speile***, The Official Publication of the Olympic Games of Munich, verlegt bei, proSprot Munchen, 1972.

________, ***Les Hymnes Nationaux Du Monde***, Paris: Editions Musicales Aug. Zurfluh, 73 Boulevard Raspail, 75006, with harmonic notation by Gerard Spiers.

________, ***The Lillehammer Olympic Arts Festival Program***

________, ***Listen to Norway—Musical Review***, Number 2, 1993.

Lists:

Olympic Music
Music Melt the Snow, Jan E. Hansen
Olympic Games in Folklore and Fine Arts, Oyvind Thorsen
A Modern Shaman, Linn Ullmann
Joiks and Jokes, Hansen
Operatic Mysteries, Oyvind Norheim
Bringing Munch Alive, Martin Anderson
Young Veteran, Terje Mosnes
Beautiful Song, Jostein Pedersen
The Extended Olympic Concept, Ivar Eskeland
The Sound of Norway, Earle Hyman
Come Blow your Horn, Tom Brevik
A Man And His Piano, Mona Levin
Vibrant Folk Music, Halgrim Berg

________, ***Mexico 1968 Programa cultural de la XIV Olimpiada***

________, ***Olympia: Journal of the Musical Competitions***, Salzburg: International Music Festival Co., 1950.

________, ***Olympic Charter 1985***, p. 32

Bulletins of the International Olympic Committee

No. 46, 1954, pp. 66–68
No. 49, 1955, p. 25
No. 50, 1955, pp. 19–20
No. 51, 1955, pp. 17–22
No. 52, 1955, pp. 17, 41, 42
No. 54, 1956, p. 29
No. 78, 1962, pp. 37, 38, 72

Musical References found in the Official Reports of the Games

Athens, 1896: p.40
London, 1908: p.48
Stockholm, 1912: pp. 308–322
Antwerp, 1920: pp. 50–51
Paris, 1924: pp. 81, 85
Amsterdam, 1928: pp. 105–107, 295, 297
Los Angeles, 1932: pp. 180–184
Lake Placid, 1932: p. 131
Berlin, 1936: vol. 1, pp. 121–124, 504–506
Garmisch, 1936: pp. 276, 284, 285
London, 1948: pp. 199, 202, 203, 207, 208, 538–540
Helsinki, 1952: pp. 106–109
Oslo, 1952: pp. 172, 173
Melbourne, 1956: pp. 97, 98
Cortina, 1956 : pp. 220, 221, 223
Stockholm, 1956: p. 64
Rome, 1960: pp. 303–305, 560, 561
Squaw Valley, 1960: pp. 53, 55, 57–60
Tokyo, 1964: pp. 221–224, 229, 233–240
Innsbruck, 1964: pp. 332, 334–336
Mexico, 1968: vol. 3, chapters on opening and closing ceremonies
Munich, 1972: vol. 1, pp. 77, 80, 82–87
Sapporo, 1972: pp. 168, 170, 172, 174, 176, 178, 181, 182, 184, 186–207
Montreal, 1976: pp. 298–300, 302, 303, 305, 306, 309, 311, 313
Innsbruck, 1976: pp. 218–220
Moscow, 1980: pp. 280, 283, 288, 294, 297–299, 301, 305, 306
Lake Placid, 1980: pp. 82, 86–91
Los Angeles, 1984: organization volume, chapter on ceremonies
Sarajevo, 1984: p. 188
Seoul, 1988
Calgary, 1988
Barcelona, 1992
Albertville, 1992
Lillehammer, 1994